Ik. Marvel

Dream life : Fable of the Seasons

Ik. Marvel
Dream life : Fable of the Seasons
ISBN/EAN: 9783744789622

Printed in Europe, USA, Canada, Australia, Japan

Cover: Foto ©Lupo / pixelio.de

More available books at **www.hansebooks.com**

DREAM LIFE:

A

FABLE OF THE SEASONS.

By Ik. Marvel.

*—— We are such stuff
As dreams are made of, and our little life
Is rounded with a sleep.*—TEMPEST.

A NEW EDITION.

NEW YORK
SCRIBNER, ARMSTRONG & CO.,
1876.

Entered, according to Act of Congress, in the year 1863, by
CHARLES SCRIBNER,
In the Clerk's Office of the District Court of the United States for the Southern District of New York.

JOHN F. TROW & SON,
PRINTERS AND BOOKBINDERS,
205-213 *East 12th St.*,
NEW YORK.

A NEW PREFACE.

TWELVE years ago, this autumn, when I had finished the concluding chapters of this little book, I wrote a letter of Dedication to Washington Irving, and forwarding it by mail to Sunnyside, begged his permission to print it. I think I shall gratify a rational curiosity of my readers (however much they may condemn my vanity) if I give his reply in full:

"MY DEAR SIR,
"Though I have a great disinclination in
" general to be the object of literary oblations and
" compliments, yet in the present instance, I have
" enjoyed your writings with such peculiar relish,
" and been so drawn toward the author by the
" qualities of head and heart evinced in them, that

A NEW PREFACE.

"I confess I feel gratified by a dedication, over
"flattering as I may deem it, which may serve as
"an outward sign that we are cordially linked to-
"gether in sympathies and friendship.

"I would only suggest that in your dedication
"you would omit the LL.D., a learned dignity
"urged upon me very much 'against the stomach
"of my sense,' and to which I have never laid
"claim.

    "Ever, my dear Sir,
     "Yours, very truly,
      " WASHINGTON IRVING.
"SUNNYSIDE, *Nov.* 1851."

I had been personally presented to Mr.
Irving for the first time, only a year before,
under the introduction of my good friend,
Mr. Clark (the veteran Editor of the old
Knickerbocker in its palmy days). Thereafter I had met him from time to time, and
had paid a charming visit to his delightful
home of Sunnyside. But it was after the date
of the publication of this book, and during
the summer of 1852, that I saw Mr. Irving
more familiarly, and came to appreciate more
fully that charming *bonhomie*, and geniality
in his character, which we all recognize so

A NEW PREFACE.

constantly in his writings. And if I set down here a few recollections of that pleasant intercourse, they will, I am sure, more than make good the place of the old letter of Dedication, and will serve to keep alive the association I wish to cherish, between my little book, and the name of the distinguished author who so kindly showed me his favor.

For the first time, after many years, Mr. Irving made a stay of a few weeks at Saratoga, in the summer of 1852 : by good fortune, I chanced to occupy a room upon the same corridor of the hotel, within a few doors of his, and shared very many of his early morning walks to the "Spring." What at once struck me very forcibly in the course of these walks, was the rare alertness and minuteness of his observation; not a fair young face could dash past us in its drapery of muslin, but the eye of the old gentleman drank in all its freshness and beauty, with the keen appetite and the grateful admiration of a boy; not a dowager brushed past us bedizened with finery, but he fastened the apparition in my memory, with some piquant remark—as the pin of an entomologist fastens a gaudy fly. No rheumatic old hero-invalid, battered in long wars with the doctors,—no droll marplot of a boy, could appear within range, but I could see in the changeful expression of my companion, the admeasurement and quiet adjustment of the appeal which either made upon his sympathy, or his humor. A flower, a tree, a burst of music, a country marketman hoist upon his wagon of cabbages—all these by turns caught and engaged his attention, however little they might interrupt the flow of his talk.

I ventured to ask on one occasion, if he had depended solely upon his memory for the thousand little descriptions of natural objects which occur in his books.

"Not wholly," he replied; and went on to tell me it had been his way in the earlier days of his authorship, to carry little tablets with him into the country, and whenever he saw a scene specially picturesque—a cottage of marked features, a noticeable tree, any picture, in short, which promised service to him,— to note down its distinguishing points, and hold it in reserve.

"This," said he, "is one among those small arts and industries, which a person who writes much, must avail himself of: they are equivalent to the little thumb sketches from which a painter makes up his larger compositions."

On our way to the church on a certain Sunday morning, he tapped my shoulder as we entered the little gate, and called my attention to a lithe young Indian girl, who had strolled down from the campment on the plains, and was standing proudly erect upon the church porch, with finger to her lips, scanning curiously the worshippers as they passed in.

"What a splendid figure of a woman!" said he: "she is puzzling over the extravagances and devotions of the white-faces."

The black, straight elf-locks, the swart face, the great wondering eye, with the gay blanket, short gown of woollen-stuff, and brilliant moccasins, made a striking picture to be sure; and I could not help thinking, that if the apparition had chanced upon him earlier, she might have figured in some story of Pokanoket or of the Prairies.

I took occasion one morning to ask if he was always able to control the "humors of writing," and to put himself resolutely to work, whatever might be the state of his feeling.

"No," he said very decidedly,—"unfortunately I cannot: there are men who do, I believe: I always envied them; but there was a period of a month or more, after I had finally decided upon literary labors, and had declined a lucrative position under Government, when it seemed as if I was utterly bereft of all the fancies I ever had; for weeks I could do nothing; but at last the clouds lifted, and I wrote off the first numbers of the Sketch-Book, and despatched to my good friends in this country, to make the most of. I feared it would not be much.

"And the worst of it is," continued he

"the good people do not allow for these periods of depression; if a man does a thing tolerably well in his happy moods, they see no reason why he should not be always in a happy mood."

I asked if he had never found relief and a stimulant to work, in the reading aloud of some favorite old author?

"Often," said he, "and none are more effective with me for this service than the sacred writers; I think I have waked a good many sleeping fancies, by the reading of a chapter in Isaiah."

In answer to inquiries of mine in regard to the incomplete state of several of the stories of Wolfert's Roost, he said, "Yes, we do not get through all we lay out. Some of those sketches had lain in my mind for a great many years; they made a sort of garret trumpery, of which I thought I would make a general clearance, leaving the odds and ends to take care of themselves.

"There was a novel too, I once laid out, in which an English lad, being a son of one of the old Regicide Judges, was to come over to New England in search of his father: he was to meet with a throng of adventures, and to arrive at length upon a Saturday night, in the midst of a terrible thunder storm, at the house of a stern old Massachusetts Puritan, who comes out to answer to the rappings; and by a flash of lightning which gleams upon the harsh, iron visage of the old man, the son fancies he recognizes his father."

And as he told it, the old gentleman wrinkled his brow, and tried to put on the fierce look he would describe.

"It's all there is of it," said he. "If you want to make a story, you can furbish it up."

There were among other notable people at Saratoga, during the summer of which I speak, the well-known Mrs. Dr. R——, of Philadelphia, since deceased,—a woman of great eccentricities, but of a wonderfully masculine mind, and of great cultivation. It was a fancy of hers to give special, social patronage to foreign artists: and among those just then at Saratoga, and the recipients of her favor, were a distinguished violinist—whose name I do not now recall—and the newly married Mme. Alboni. Mr. Irving, in common with her other acquaintances, she was inclined to make contributory to her attentions. To this Mr. Irving was not averse—both from his extreme love of music, and his kindliness toward the artists themselves; yet, in his own quiet way, I think he fretted considerably at being pounced upon at odd hours to give them French talk.

"It's very awkward," said he to me one day; "I have had large occasion for practice to be sure; but I rather fancy after all—our own language; it's heartier and easier."

He was utterly incapable of being lionized; time and again, under the trees in the court of the hotel, did I hear him enter upon some pleasant story, lighted up with that rare turn of his eye, and by his deft expressions, when as chance acquaintances grouped about him— as is the way of Watering Places—and eager listeners multiplied, his hilarity and spirit took a chill from the increasing auditory, and drawing abruptly to a close, he would sidle away with a friend, and be gone.

Among the visitors was a tall, interesting young girl—from Louisiana, if I mistake not —who had the reputation of being a great heiress, and who was, of course, beset by a host of admirers. There was something very attractive in her air, and Mr. Irving was never tired of gazing on her, as she walked, with what he called a " faun-like step," across the lawn, or up and down the corridors. Her eyes too—" dove-like," he termed them—were his special admiration. He watched with an amused interest the varying fortunes of the rival lovers, and often met me with—" Well, who is in favor to-day?" And he discussed very freely the varying chances.

One brusque, heavy man, who thought to carry the matter through by a *coup de main*, he was sure could never succeed. A second who was most assiduous, but whose brazen confidence was unyielding, he counted still less upon. But a quiet, somewhat older gentleman, whose look was ever full of tender appeal, and who bore himself with a modest dignity, he reckoned the probable winner. "He will feel a Nay grievously," said he; "but for the others, they will forget it in a supper."

I believe it eventually proved that no one of those present was the successful suitor. I know only that the fair girl was afterward a bride; and (what we all so little anticipated) her home is now a scene of desolation, her fortune very likely a wreck, her family scattered or slain, and herself—maybe, a fugitive.

I saw Mr. Irving afterward repeatedly in New York, and passed two delightful days at Sunnyside. I can never forget a drive with him upon a crisp autumn morning through Sleepy Hollow, and all the notable localities of his neighborhood, in the course of which he kindly called my attention in the most unaffected and incidental way to those which nad been specially illustrated by his pen; and with a rare humor recounted to me some of his boyish adventures among the old Dutch farmers of this region. Most of all, it is impossible for me to forget the rare kindliness of his manner, his friendly suggestions, and the beaming expression of his eye.

I met it last, at the little stile, from which I strolled away to the station at Dearman; and when I saw the kind face again, it was in the coffin, at the little church, where he attended service. But the eyes were closed, and the wonderful radiance of expression—gone. It seemed to me that death never took away more from a living face; it was but a cold shadow lying there, of the man who had taught a nation to love him.

EDGEWOOD, *Sept.* 1868.

CONTENTS.

INTRODUCTORY.

	PAGE
I. WITH MY AUNT TABITHY,	13
II. WITH MY READER,	21

DREAMS OF BOYHOOD.

SPRING, ... 38
   I. RAIN IN THE GARRET, . 88
   II. SCHOOL DREAMS, ... 45
   III. BOY SENTIMENT, ... 55
   IV. A FRIEND MADE AND FRIEND LOST, . . 61
   V. BOY RELIGION, ... 72
   VI. A NEW ENGLAND SQUIRE, ... 79
   VII. THE COUNTRY CHURCH, ... 90
   VIII. A HOME SCENE, ... 93

DREAMS OF YOUTH.

SUMMER, ... 109
   I. CLOISTER LIFE, ... 115
   II. FIRST AMBITION, ... 126

	PAGE
III. COLLEGE ROMANCE,	131
IV. FIRST LOOK AT THE WORLD,	142
V. A BROKEN HOME,	152
VI. FAMILY CONFIDENCE,	161
VII. A GOOD WIFE,	163
VIII. A BROKEN HOPE,	176

DREAMS OF MANHOOD.

AUTUMN,	187
I. PRIDE OF MANLINESS,	192
II. MAN OF THE WORLD,	199
III. MANLY HOPE,	206
IV. MANLY LOVE,	215
V. CHEER AND CHILDREN,	221
VI. DREAM OF DARKNESS,	229
VII. PEACE,	237

DREAMS OF AGE.

WINTER,	247
I. WHAT IS GONE,	251
II. WHAT IS LEFT,	257
III. GRIEF AND JOY OF AGE,	263
IV. THE END OF DREAMS,	269

INTRODUCTORY.

I.

With my Aunt Tabithy.

PSHAW !- -said my Aunt Tabithy,—have you not done with dreaming ?

My Aunt Tabithy, though an excellent and most notable person, loves occasionally a quiet bit of satire. And when I told her that I was sharpening my pen for a new story of those dreamy fancies, and half experiences, which lie grouped along the journeying hours of my solitary life, she smiled as if in derision.

——" Ah, Isaac," said she, " all that is exhausted : you have rung so many changes on your hopes and your dreams, that you have nothing left, but to make them real——if you can."

It is very idle to get angry with a good-natured old lady : I did better than this :—I made her listen to me.

——Exhausted, do you say, Aunt Tabithy? Is life then exhausted, is hope gone out, is fancy dead?

No, no. Hope and the world are full; and he who drags into book-pages a phase or two of the great life of passion, of endurance, of love, of sorrow, is but wetting a feather in the sea that breaks ceaselessly along the great shore of the years. Every man's heart is a living drama; every death is a drop-scene; every book only a faint foot-light to throw a little flicker on the stage.

There is no need of wandering widely, to catch incident or adventure: they are everywhere about us; each day is a succession of escapes and joys;— not perhaps clear to the world, but brooding in our thought, and living in our brain. From the very first, Angels and Devils are busy with us, and we are struggling against them, and for them.

No, no, Aunt Tabithy,—this life of musing does not exhaust so easily. It is like the springs of the farm-land, that are fed with all the showers and the dews of the year, and that from the narrow fissures of the rock, send up streams continually:—or it is like the deep well in the meadow, where one may see stars at noon——when no stars are shining.

What is Reverie, and what are these Day-dreams, but fleecy cloud-drifts that float eternally, and eternally change shapes, upon the great overarching sky of thought? You may seize the strong outlines that the passion breezes of to-day shall throw into their figures; but to-morrow may breed a whirlwind that will chase swift, gigantic shadows over the heaven of your thought, and change the whole landscape of your life.

Dream-land will never be exhausted, until we enter the land of dreams; and until, in "shuffling off this mortal coil," thought will become fact, and all facts will be only thought.

As it is, I can conceive no mood of mind more in keeping with what is to follow upon the grave, than those fancies which warp our frail hulks toward the ocean of the Infinite; and that so sublimate the realities of this being, that they seem to belong to that shadowy realm, where every day's journey is leading.

It was warm weather; and my aunt was dozing. "What is this all to be about?" said she, recovering her knitting needle.

"About love, and toil, and duty, and sorrow," said I.

My aunt laid down her knitting, looked at me over the rim of her spectacles, and——took snuff.

I said nothing.

"How many times have you been in love, Isaac?" said she.

It was now my turn to say——"Pshaw!"

Judging from her look of assurance, I could not possibly have made a more satisfactory reply.

My aunt finished the needle she was upon— smoothed the stocking leg over her knee, and looking at me with a very comical expression, said,— "Isaac, you are a sad fellow!"

I did not like the tone of this: it sounded very much as if it would have been in the mouth of any one else——' bad fellow.'

And she went on to ask me in a very bantering way if my stock of youthful loves was not nearly exhausted; and she cited the episode of the fair-haired Enrica, as perhaps the most tempting that I could draw from my experience.

A better man than myself,—if he had only a fair share of vanity,—would have been nettled at this; and I replied somewhat tartly, that I had never professed to write my experiences. These might be more or less tempting; but certainly, if they were of a kind which I have attempted to portray in the characters of Bella, or of Carry, neither my Aunt Tabithy nor any one else, should have heard such truth from any book of mine. There are griefs too sacred to be babbled to the world; and there may be loves, which one would forbear to whisper even to a friend.

No, no,—imagination has been playing pranks with memory; and if I have made the feeling real, I am content that the facts should be false. Feeling indeed has a higher truth in it, than circumstance. It appeals to a larger jury for acquittal: it is approved or condemned by a better judge. And if I can catch this bolder and richer truth of feeling, I will not mind if the types of it are all fabrications.

If I run over some sweet experience of love, (my Aunt Tabithy brightened a little) must I make good the fact that the loved one lives, and expose her name and qualities, to make your sympathy sound? Or shall I not rather be working upon higher and holier ground, if I take the passion for itself, and so weave it into words, that you, and every willing sufferer may recognize the fervor, and forget the personality?

Life after all is but a bundle of hints, each suggesting actual and positive development, but rarely reaching it. And as I recal these hints, and in fancy, trace them to their issues, I am as truly dealing with life, as if my life had dealt them all the same.

This is what I would be doing in the present book;—I would catch up here and there the shreds of feeling which the brambles and roughnesses of the world have left tangling on my heart, and weave them out into those soft and perfect tissues which—if the world had been only a little less rough,—might now perhaps enclose my heart altogether.

"Ah," said my Aunt Tabithy, as she smoothed the stocking leg again, with a sigh,—"there is after all but one youth-time: and if you put down its memories once, you can find no second growth."

My Aunt Tabithy was wrong. There is as much growth in the thoughts and feelings that run behind us, as in those that run before us. You may make a rich, full picture of your childhood to-day; but let the hour go by, and the darkness stoop to your pillow with its million shapes of the past, and my word for it, you shall have some flash of childhood lighten upon you, that was unknown to your busiest thought of the morning.

Let a week go by; and in some interval of care as you recal the smile of a mother, or some pale sister who is dead, a new crowd of memories will rush upon your soul, and leave their traces in such tears as will make you kinder and better for days and weeks. Or you shall assist at some neighbor funeral, where the little dead one—(like one you have seen before)—shall hold in its tiny grasp—(as you have taught little dead hands to do)—fresh flowers, laughing flowers, lying lightly on the white robe of the dear child—all pale—cold—silent——

I had touched my Aunt Tabithy: she had dropped a stitch in her knitting. I believe she was weeping.

——Aye, this brain of ours is a master-worker, whose appliances we do not one half know; and this heart of ours is a rare storehouse, furnishing the brain with new material every hour of our lives; and their limits we shall not know, until they shall end—together.

Nor is there, as many faint-hearts imagine, but one phase of earnestness in our life of feeling. One train of deep emotion cannot fill up the heart: it radiates like a star, God-ward and earth-ward. It spends and reflects all ways. Its force is to be reckoned not so much by token, as by capacity Facts are the poorest and most slumberous evi dences of passion, or of affection. True feeling is ranging everywhere; whereas your actual attachments are too apt to be tied to sense.

A single affection may indeed be true, earnest and absorbing; but such an one after all, is but a type—and if the object be worthy, a glorious type —of the great book of feeling: it is only the vapor from the cauldron of the heart, and bears no deeper relation to its exhaustless sources, than the letter which my pen makes, bears to the thought that inspires it,—or than a single morning strain of your orioles and thrushes, bears to that wide bird-chorus, which is making every sunrise—a worship, and every grove—a temple!

My Aunt Tabithy nodded.

Nor is this a mere bachelor fling against constancy. I can believe, Heaven knows, in an unalterable and unflinching affection, which neither desires nor admits the prospect of any other. But when one is tasking his brain to talk for his heart, —when he is not writing positive history, but only making mention (as it were) of the heart's capacities, who shall say that he has reached the fullness —that he has exhausted the stock of its feeling, or that he has touched its highest notes? It is true there is but one heart in a man to be stirred; but every stir creates a new combination of feeling, that like the turn of a kaleidoscope will show some fresh color, or form.

A bachelor to be sure has a marvellous advantage in this; and with the tenderest influences once anchored in the bay of marriage, there is little disposition to scud off under each pleasant breeze of feeling. Nay, I can even imagine—perhaps somewhat captiously—that after marriage, feeling would become a habit, a rich and holy habit certainly, but yet a habit, which weakens the omnivorous grasp of the affections, and schools one to a unity of emotion, that doubts and ignores the promptness and variety of impulse, which we bachelors possess.

My aunt nodded again.

Could it be that she approved what I had been saying? I hardly knew.

Poor old lady,—she did not know herself. She was asleep!

II.

With my Reader.

HAVING silenced my Aunt Tabithy, I shall be generous enough in my triumph, to offer an explanatory chat to my reader.

This is a history of Dreams; and there will be those who will sneer at such a history, as the work of a dreamer. So indeed it is; and you, my courteous reader, are a dreamer too!

You would perhaps like to find your speculations about wealth, marriage, or influence, called by some better name than Dreams. You would like to see the history of them—if written at all—baptized at the font of your own vanity, with some such title as—life's cares, or life's work.

If there had been a philosophic naming to my observations, you might have reckoned them good: as it is, you count them all bald and palpable fiction.

But is it so? I care not how matter of fact you may be, you have in your own life, at some time, proved the very truth of what I have set down : and the chances are, that even now, gray as you may be, and economic as you may be, and devotional as you pretend to be, you light up your Sabbath reflections with just such dreams of wealth, of per centages, or of family, as you will find scattered over these pages.

I am not to be put aside with any talk about stocks, and duties, and respectability : all these, though very eminent matters, are but so many types in the volume of your thought ; and your eager resolves about them, are but so many ambitious waves, breaking up from the great sea of dreamy speculation, that has spread over your soul, from its first start into the realm of CONSCIOUSNESS.

No man's brain is so dull, and no man's eye so blind, that they cannot catch food for dreams. Each little episode of life is full, had we but the perception of its fullness. There is no such thing as blank in the world of thought. Every action and emotion have their levelopment growing and gaining on the soul. Every affection has its tears and smiles. Nay, the very material world is full of meaning, and by suggesting thought, is making us what we are, and what we will be.

The sparrow that is twittering on the edge of my balcony, is calling up to me this moment, a world of memories that reach over half my life time, and a world of hope that stretches farther than any flight of sparrows. The rose-tree which shades his mottled coat is full of buds and blossoms; and each bud and blossom is a token of promise, that has issues covering life, and reaching beyond death. The quiet sunshine beyond the flower and beyond the sparrow,—glistening upon the leaves, and playing in delicious waves of warmth over the reeking earth, is lighting both heart and hope, and quickening into activity a thousand thoughts of what has been, and of what will be. The meadow stretching away under its golden flood—waving with grain, and with the feathery blossoms of the grass, and golden butter cups, and white, nodding daisies, comes to my eye like the lapse of fading childhood,—studded here and there with the bright blossoms of joy, crimsoned all over with the flush of health, and enamelled with memories that perfume the soul. The blue hills beyond, with deep blue shadows gathered in their bosoms, lie before me like mountains of years, over which I shall climb through shadows to the slope of Age, and go down to the deeper shadows of Death.

Nor are dreams without their variety, whatever your character may be. I care not how much, in the pride of your practical judgment, or in your learned fancies, you may sneer at any dream of love, and reckon it all a poet's fiction: there are times when such dreams come over you like a summer cloud, and almost stifle you with their warmth.

Seek as you will for increase of lands or moneys, and there are moments when a spark of some giant mind will flash over your cravings, and wake your soul suddenly to a quick, and yearning sense of that influence which is begotten of intellect; and you task your dreams—as I have copied them here —to build before you the pleasures of such a renown.

I care not how worldly you may be: there are times when all distinctions seem like dust, and when at the graves of the great, you dream of a coming country, where your proudest hopes shall be dimmed forever.

Married or unmarried, young or old, poet or worker, you are still a dreamer, and will one time know, and feel, that your life is but a dream. Yet you call this fiction: you stave off the thoughts in print which come over you in reverie. You will not admit to the eye what is true to the heart. Poor weakling, and worldling,—you are not strong enough to face yourself!

You will read perhaps with smiles: you will possibly praise the ingenuity: you will talk, with a lip schooled against the slightest quiver, of some bit of pathos, and say that it is—well done. Yet why is it well done?—only because it is stolen from your very life and heart. It is good, because it is so common:—ingenious, because it is so honest:—well-conceived, because it is not conceived at all.

There are thousands of mole-eyed people, who count all passion in print—a lie:—people who will grow into a rage at trifles, and weep in the dark, and love in secret, and hope without mention, and cover it all under the cloak of what they call—

propriety. I can see before me now some gray-haired old gentleman, very money-getting, very correct, very cleanly, who reads the morning paper with unction, and his Bible with determination: who listens to dull sermons with patience, and who prays with quiet self-applause,—and yet there are moments belonging to his life, when his curdled affections yearn for something that they have not, when his avarice oversteps all the commandments, —when his pride builds castles full of splendor; and yet put this before his eye, and he reads with the most careless air in the world, and condemns as arrant fiction, what cannot be proved to the elders.

We do not like to see our emotions unriddled it is not agreeable to the proud man to find his weaknesses exposed: it is shocking to the disappointed lover to see his heart laid bare: it is a great grief to the pining maiden to witness the exposure of her loves. We do not like our fancies painted: we do not contrive them for rehearsal · our dreams are private, and when they are made public, we disown them.

I sometimes think that I must be a very honest fellow, for writing down those fancies which every one else seems afraid to whisper. I shall at least come in for my share of the odium in entertaining such fancies: indeed, I shall expect the charge of entertaining them exclusively; and shall scarce expect to find a single fellow-confessor, unless it be some pure, and innocent thoughted girl, who will say *peccavi*, to—here and there—a single rainbow fancy.

Well, I can bear it; but in bearing it, I shall be consoled with the reflection that I have a great company of fellow-sufferers, who lack only the honesty to tell me of their sympathy. It will even relieve in no small degree my burden, to watch the effort they will take to conceal, what I have so boldly divulged.

Nature is very much the same thing in one man, that it is in another: and as I have already said, Feeling has a higher truth in it, than circumstance. Let it only be touched fairly and honestly, and the heart of humanity answers; but if it be touched foully or one-sidedly, you may find here and there a lame-souled creature who will give response, but there is no heart throb in it.

Of one thing I am sure:—if my pictures are fair, worthy, and hearty, you *must* see it in the reading: but if they are forced and hard, no amount of kindness can make you feel their truth as I want them felt.

I make no self-praise out of this: if feeling has been honestly set down, it is only in virtue of a native impulse, over which I have altogether too little control; but if it is set down badly, I have wronged Nature, and (as Nature is kind) I have wronged myself.

A great many inquisitive people will, I do not doubt, be asking after all this prelude, if my pictures are true pictures? The question,—the court cous reader will allow me to say,—is an impertinent one. It is but a shabby truth that wants an author's affidavit to make it trust-worthy. I shall not help my story by any such poor support. If there are not enough elements of truth, honesty and nature in my pictures, to make them believed, they shall have no oath of mine to bolster them up.

I have been a sufferer in this way before now; and a little book that I had the whim to publish a year since, has been set down by many as an arrant piece of imposture. Claiming sympathy as a Bachelor, I have been recklessly set down as a cold, undeserving man of family! My story of troubles and loves has been sneered at, as the sheerest gammon.

But among this crowd of cold-blooded critics, it was pleasant to hear of one or two pursy old fellows who railed at me, for winning the affections of a sweet Italian girl, and then leaving her to pine in discontent! Yet in the face of this, an old companion of mine in Rome, with whom I accidentally met the other day,—wondered how on earth I could have made so tempting a story out of the matronly and black-haired spinster, with whom I happened to be quartered in the Eternal City!

I shall leave my critics to settle such differences between themselves; and consider it far better to bear with slanders from both sides of the house, than to bewray the pretty tenderness of the pursy old gentlemen, or to cast a doubt upon the practical testimony of my quondam companion. Both give me high and judicious compliment—all the more grateful because only half deserved. For I never yet was conscious—alas, that the confession should be forced from me!—of winning the heart of any maiden whether native, or Italian; and as for such delicacy of imagination as to work up a lovely damsel out of the withered remnant that forty odd years of Italian life can spare, I can assure my middle-aged friends, (and it may serve as a *caveat*) —I can lay no claim to it whatever.

The trouble has been, that those who have believed one passage have discredited another; and those who have sympathized with me in trifles, have deserted me when affairs grew earnest. I have had sympathy enough with my married griefs; but when it came to the perplexing torments of my single life——not a weeper could I find!

I would suggest to those who intend to believe only half of my present book, that they exercise a little discretion in their choice. I am not fastidious in the matter; and only ask them to believe what counts most toward the goodness of humanity, and to discredit—if they will persist in it—only what tells badly for our common nature. The man or the woman who believes well, is apt to work well; and Faith is as much the key to happiness here, as it is the key to happiness hereafter.

I have only one thing more to say, before I get upon my story. A great many sharp-eyed people who have a horror of light reading—by which they mean whatever does not make mention of stocks, cottons, or moral homilies,—will find much fault with my book for its ephemeral character.

I am sorry that I cannot gratify such: homilies are not at all in my habit; and it does seem to me an exhausting way of disposing of a good moral, to hammer it down to a single point, so that there shall be only one chance of driving it home. For my own part, I count it a great deal better philosophy to fuse it, and rarify it, so that it shall spread out into every crevice of a story, and give a color and a taste, as it were, to the whole mass.

I know there are very good people, who, if they cannot lay their finger on so much doctrine set down in old fashioned phrase, will never get an inkling of it at all. With such people, goodness is a thing of understanding, more than of feeling; and all their morality has its action in the brain.

God forbid that I should sneer at this terrible infirmity, which Providence has seen fit to inflict: God forbid too, that I should not be grateful to the same kind Providence, for bestowing upon others among his creatures a more genial apprehension of true goodness, and a hearty sympathy with every shade of human kindness.

But in all this, I am not making out a case for my own correct teaching, or insinuating the propriety of my tone. I shall leave the book in this regard, to speak for itself; and whoever feels himself growing worse for the reading, I advise to lay it down. It will be very harmless on the shelf, however it may be in the hand.

I shall lay no claim to the title of moralist, teacher, or romancist;—my thoughts start pleasant pictures to my mind; and in a garrulous humor I put my finger in the button-hole of my indulgent friend,—and tell him some of them—giving him leave to quit me whenever he chooses.

Or, if a lady is my listener, let her fancy me only an honest, simple-hearted fellow, whose familiarities are so innocent that she can pardon them;— taking her hand in his, and talking on;—sometimes looking in her eyes, and then looking into the sunshine for relief;—sometimes prosy with narrative, and then sharpening up my matter with a few touches of honest pathos;—let her imagine this, I say, and we may become the most excellent friends in the world.

Spring;

OR,

DREAMS OF BOYHOOD.

DREAMS OF BOYHOOD

Spring.

THE old chroniclers made the year begin in the season of frosts; and they have launched us upon the current of the months, from the snowy banks of January. I love better to count time, from spring to spring; it seems to me far more cheerful, to reckon the year by blossoms, than by blight.

Bernardin de St. Pierre, in his sweet story of Virginia, makes the bloom of the cocoa-tree, or the growth of the banana, a yearly and a loved monitor of the passage of her life. How cold and cheerless in the comparison, would be the icy chronology of the North;——So many years have I seen the lakes locked, and the foliage die!

The budding and blooming of spring, seem to belong properly to the opening of the months. It is the season of the quickest expansion, of the warmest blood, of the readiest growth; it is the boy-age of the year. The birds sing in chorus in the spring—just as children prattle; the brooks run full—like the overflow of young hearts; the showers drop easily—as young tears flow; and the whole sky is as capricious as the mind of a boy.

Between tears and smiles, the year, like the child, struggles into the warmth of life. The old year,—say what the chronologists will,—lingers upon the very lap of spring; and is only fairly gone, when the blossoms of April have strewn their pall of glory upon his tomb, and the blue-birds have chanted his requiem.

It always seems to me as if an access of life came with the melting of the winter's snows; and as if every rootlet of grass that lifted its first green blade from the matted debris of the old year's decay, bore my spirit upon it, nearer to the largess of Heaven.

I love to trace the break of spring step by step: I love even those long rain-storms that sap the icy fortresses of the lingering winter,—that melt the snows upon the hills, and swell the mountain-brooks;—that make the pools heave up their glassy cerements of ice, and hurry down the crashing fragments into the wastes of ocean.

I love the gentle thaws that you can trace, day by day, by the stained snow-banks, shrinking from the grass; and by the gentle drip of the cottage-caves. I love to search out the sunny slopes by a southern wall, where the reflected sun does double duty to the earth, and where the frail anemone, or the faint blush of the arbutus, in the midst of the bleak March atmosphere, will touch your heart, like a hope of Heaven, in a field of graves! Later come those soft, smoky days, when the patches of winter grain show green under the shelter of leafless woods, and the last snow-drifts, reduced to shrunken skeletons of ice, lie upon the slopes of northern hills, leaking away their life.

Then, the grass at your door grows into the color of the sprouting grain, and the buds upon the lilacs swell, and burst. The peaches bloom upon the wall, and the plums wear bodices of white. The sparkling oriole picks string for his hammock on the sycamore, and the sparrows twitter in pairs. The old elms throw down their dingy flowers, and color their spray with green; and the brooks, where you throw your worm or the minnow, float down whole fleets of the crimson blossoms of the maple. Finally, the oaks step into the opening quadrille of spring, with greyish tufts of a modest verdure, which, by and by, will be long and glossy leaves. The dog-wood pitches his broad, white tent, in the edge of the forest; the dandelions lie along the hillocks, like stars in a sky of green; and the wild cherry, growing in all the hedge-rows, without other culture than God's, lifts up to Him, thankfully, its tremulous white fingers.

Amid all this, come the rich rains of spring. The ₋ffections of a boy grow up with tears to water them; and the year blooms with showers. But the clouds hover over an April sky, timidly—like shadows upon innocence. The showers come gently, and drop daintily to the earth,—with now and then a glimpse of sunshine to make the drops bright—like so many tears of joy.

The rain of winter is cold, and it comes in bitter scuds that blind you; but the rain of April steals upon you coyly, half reluctantly,—yet lovingly—like the steps of a bride to the Altar.

It does not gather like the storm-clouds of winter, grey and heavy along the horizon, and creep with subtle and insensible approaches (like age) to the very zenith; but there are a score of white-winged swimmers afloat, that your eye has chased, as you lay fatigued with the delicious languor of an April sun;—nor have you scarce noticed that a little bevy of those floating clouds had grouped together in a sombre company. But presently, you see across the fields, the dark grey streaks stretching like lines of mists from the green bosom of the valley, to that spot of sky where the company of clouds is loitering; and with an easy shifting of the helm, the fleet of swimmers come drifting over you, and drop their burden into the dancing pools, and make the flowers ·glisten, and the eaves drip with their crystal bounty.

The cattle linger still, cropping the new-come grass; and childhood laughs joyously at the warm rain ;—or under the cottage roof, catches with eager ear, the patter of its fall.

——And with that patter on the roof,—so like to the patter of childish feet—my story of boyish dreams shall begin.

I.

Rain in the Garret.

IT is an old garret with big, brown rafters; and the boards between are stained darkly with the rain-storms of fifty years. And as the sportive April shower quickens its flood, it seems as if its torrents would come dashing through the shingles, upon you, and upon your play. But it will not: for you know that the old roof is strong; and that it has kept you, and all that love you, for long years from the rain, and from the cold: you know that the hardest storms of winter will only make a little oozing leak, that trickles down the brown stains, —like tears.

You love that old garret roof; and you nestle down under its slope, with a sense of its protecting power that no castle walls can give to your maturer years. Aye, your heart clings in boyhood to the roof-tree of the old family garret, with a grateful affection, and an earnest confidence, that the after years—whatever may be their successes, or their honors—can never re-create. Under the roof-tree of his home, the boy feels SAFE : and where, in the whole realm of life, with its bitter toils, and its bitterer temptations, will he feel *safe* again ?

But this you do not know. It seems only a grand old place; and it is capital fun to search in its corners, and drag out some bit of quaint old furniture, with a leg broken, and lay a cushion across it, and fix your reins upon the lion's claws of the feet, and then—gallop away! And you offer sister Nelly a chance, if she will be good; and throw out very patronizing words to little Charlie, who is mounted upon a much humbler horse,—to wit, a decrepid nursery-chair,—as he of right should be, since he is three years your junior.

I know no nobler forage ground for a romantic, venturesome, mischievous boy, than the garret of an old family mansion, on a day of storm. It is a perfect field of chivalry. The heavy rafters, the dashing rain, the piles of spare mattresses to carouse upon, the big trunks to hide in, the old white coats and hats hanging in obscure corners, like ghosts—are great! And it is so far away from the old lady, who keeps rule in the nursery, that there is no possible risk of a scolding, for twisting off the fringe of the rug. There is no baby in the garret to wake up. There is no 'company' in the garret to be disturbed by the noise. There is no crotchety

old Uncle, or Grand Ma, with their everlasting—
"Boys—boys!"—and then a look of such horror!

There is great fun in groping through a tall barrel of books and pamphlets, on the look-out for startling pictures; and there are chestnuts in the garret, drying, which you have discovered on a ledge of the chimney; and you slide a few into your pocket, and munch them quietly,—giving now and then one to Nelly, and begging her to keep silent—for you have a great fear of its being forbidden fruit.

Old family garrets have their stocks, as I said, of cast-away clothes, of twenty years gone by; and it is rare sport to put them on; buttoning in a pillow or two for the sake of good fulness; and then to trick out Nelly in some strange-shaped head-gear, and old-fashioned brocade petticoat caught up with pins; and in such guise, to steal cautiously down stairs, and creep slily into the sitting-room,—half afraid of a scolding, and very sure of good fun;—trying to look very sober, and yet almost ready to die with the laugh that you know you will make. And your mother tries to look harshly at little Nelly for putting on her grandmother's best bonnet; but Nelly's laughing eyes forbid it utterly; and the mother spoils all her scolding with a perfect shower of kisses.

After this, you go marching, very stately, into the nursery; and utterly amaze the old nurse and make a deal of wonderment for the staring, half-frightened baby, who drops his rattle, and makes a bob at you, as if he would jump into your waistcoat pocket.

But you grow tired of this; you tire even of the swing, and of the pranks of Charlie; and you glide away into a corner, with an old, dog's-eared copy of Robinson Crusoe. And you grow heart and soul into the story, until you tremble for the poor fellow with his guns, behind the palisade; and are yourself half dead with fright, when you peep cautiously over the hill with your glass, and see the cannibals at their orgies around the fire.

Yet, after all, you think the old fellow must have had a capital time, with a whole island to himself; and you think you would like such a time yourself, if only Nelly, and Charlie, could be there with you. But this thought does not come till afterward; for the time, you are nothing but Crusoe; you are living in his cave with Poll the parrot, and are looking out for your goats, and man Friday.

You dream what a nice thing it would be, for you to slip away some pleasant morning—not to York, as young Crusoe did, but to New York,— and take passage as a sailor; and how, if they knew you were going, there would be such a world of good-byes; and how, if they did not know it, there would be such a world of wonder!

And then the sailor's dress would be altogether such a jaunty affair; and it would be such rare sport to lie off upon the yards far aloft, as you have seen sailors in pictures, looking out upon the blue and tumbling sea. No thought now in your boyish dreams, of sleety storms, and cables stiffened with ice, and crashing spars, and great ice-bergs towering fearfully around you!

You would have better luck than even Crusoe; you would save a compass, and a Bible, and stores of hatchets, and the captain's dog, and great puncheons of sweetmeats (which Crusoe altogether overlooked); and you would save a tent or two, which you could set up on the shore, and an American flag, and a small piece of cannon, which you could fire as often as you liked. At night, you would sleep in a tree—though you wonder how Crusoe did it,—and would say the prayers you had been taught to say at home, and fall to sleep,—dreaming of Nelly and Charlie.

At sunrise, or thereabouts, you would come down, feeling very much refreshed; and make a very nice breakfast off of smoked herring and sea-bread, with a little currant jam, and a few oranges. After this you would haul ashore a chest or two of the sailors' clothes, and putting a few large jack-knives in your pocket, would take a stroll over the island, and dig a cave somewhere, and roll in a cask or two of sea-bread. And you fancy yourself growing after a time very tall and corpulent, and wearing a magnificent goat-skin cap, trimmed with green ribbons, and set off with a plume. You think you would have put a few more guns in the palisade than Crusoe did, and charged them with a little more grape.

After a long while, you fancy a ship would arrive, which would carry you back; and you count upon very great surprise on the part of your father, and little Nelly, as you march up to the door of the old family mansion, with plenty of gold in your pocket, and a small bag of cocoanuts for Charlie, and with a great deal of pleasant talk, about your island, far away in the South Seas.

— —Or, perhaps it is not Crusoe at all, that your eyes and your heart cling to, but only some little story about Paul and Virginia;—that dear little Virginia! how many tears have been shed over her—not in garrets only, or by boys only!

You would have liked Virginia—you know you would; but you perfectly hate the beldame aunt, who sent for her to come to France; you think she must have been like the old school-mistress, who occasionally boxes your ears with the cover of the spelling-book, or makes you wear one of the girls' bonnets, that smells strongly of paste-board, and calico.

As for black Domingue, you think he was a capital old fellow; and you think more of him, and his bananas, than you do of the bursting, throbbing heart of poor Paul. As yet, Dream-life does not take hold on love. A little maturity of heart is wanted, to make up what the poets call sensibility. If love should come to be a dangerous, chivalric matter, as in the case of Helen Mar and Wallace, you can very easily conceive of it, and can take hold of all the little accessories of male costume, and embroidering of banners; but as for pure sentiment, such as lies in the sweet story of Bernardin de St. Pierre, it is quite beyond you.

The rich, soft nights, in which one might doze in his hammock, watching the play of the silvery moon-beams upon the orange leaves, and upon the waves, you can understand; and you fall to dreaming of that lovely Isle of France; and wondering if Virginia did not perhaps have some relations on the island, who raise pine-apples, and such sort of things, still?

——And so, with your head upon your hand, in your quiet garret corner, over some such beguiling story, your thought leans away from the book, into your own dreamy cruise over the sea of life.

II.

School Dreams.

IT is a proud thing to go out from under the realm of a school-mistress, and to be enrolled in a company of boys who are under the guidance of a master. It is one of the earliest steps of worldly pride, which has before it a long and tedious ladder of ascent. Even the advice of the old mistress, and the nine-penny book that she thrusts into your hand as a parting gift, pass for nothing; and her kiss of adieu, if she tenders it in the sight of your fellows, will call up an angry rush of blood to the cheek, that for long years shall drown all sense of its kindness.

You have looked admiringly many a day upon the tall fellows who play at the door of Dr. Bidlow's school: you have looked with reverence, second only to that felt for the old village church, upon its dark-looking heavy brick walls. It seemed to be redolent of learning; and stopping at times, to gaze upon the gallipots and broken retorts, at the second story window, you have pondered, in your boyish way, upon the inscrutable wonders of Science, and the ineffable dignity of Dr. Bidlow's brick school!

Dr. Bidlow seems to you to belong to a race of giants; and yet he is a spare, thin man, with a hooked nose, a large, flat, gold watch-key, a crack in his voice, a wig, and very dirty wristbands. Still you stand in awe at the mere sight of him;—an awe that is very much encouraged by a report made to you by a small boy,—that "Old Bid" keeps a large ebony ruler in his desk. You are amazed at the small boy's audacity: it astonishes you that any one who had ever smelt the strong fumes of sulphur and ether in the Doctor's room, and had seen him turn red vinegar blue (as they say he does), should call him "Old Bid!"

You, however, come very little under his control; you enter upon the proud life, in the small boy's department,—under the dominion of the English master. He is a different personage from Dr. Bidlow: he is a dapper, little man, who twinkles his eye in a peculiar fashion, and who has a way of marching about the school-room with his hands crossed behind him, giving a playful flirt to his coat-tails. He wears a pen tucked behind his ear: his hair is carefully set up at the sides, and upon the top, to conceal (as you think later in life) his diminutive height; and he steps very springily around behind the benches, glancing now and then at the books,—cautioning one scholar about his dog's-ears, and startling another from a doze, by a very loud and odious snap of his forefinger upon the boy's head.

At other times he sticks a hand in the armlet of his waistcoat: he brandishes in the other a thickish bit of smooth cherry-wood,—sometimes dressing his hair withal; and again, giving his head a slight scratch behind the ear, while he takes occasion at the same time, for an oblique glance at a fat boy in the corner, who is reaching down from his seat after a little paper pellet, that has just been discharged at him from some unknown quarter. The master steals very cautiously and quickly to the rear of the stooping boy,—dreadfully exposed by his unfortunate position,—and inflicts a stinging blow. A weak-eyed little scholar on the next bench ventures a modest titter; at which the assistant makes a significant motion with his ruler—on the seat, as it were, of an imaginary pair of pantaloons,—which renders the weak-eyed boy on a sudden, very insensible to the recent joke.

You, meantime, profess to be very much engrossed with your grammar—turned upside down: you think it must have hurt; and are only sorry that it did not happen to a tall, dark-faced boy who cheated you in a swop of jack-knives. You innocently think that he must be a very bad boy, and fancy—aided by a suggestion of the old nurse at home, on the same point,—that he will one day come to the gallows.

There is a platform on one side of the school-room, where the teacher sits at a little red table, and they have a tradition among the boys, that a pin properly bent, was one day put into the chair of the English master, and that he did not wear his hand in the armlet of his waistcoat, for two whole days thereafter. Yet his air of dignity seems proper enough in a man of such erudition, and such grasp of imagination, as he must possess. For he can quote poetry,—some of the big scholars have heard him do it:—he can parse the whole of Paradise Lost; and he can cipher in Long Division, and the Rule of Three, as if it was all Simple Addition; and then—such a hand as he writes, and such a superb capital B! It is hard to understand how he does it.

Sometimes, lifting the lid of your desk, where you pretend to be very busy with your papers, you steal the reading of some brief passage of Lazy Lawrence, or of the Hungarian Brothers, and muse about it for hours afterward, to the great detriment of your ciphering; or, deeply lost in the story of the Scottish Chiefs, you fall to comparing such villains as Monteith with the stout boys who tease you; and you only wish they could come within reach of the fierce Kirkpatrick's claymore.

But you are frighted out of this stolen reading by a circumstance that stirs your young blood very strangely. The master is looking very sourly on a certain morning, and has caught sight of the little weak-eyed boy over beyond you, reading Roderick

Random. He sends out for a long birch rod, and having trimmed off the leaves carefully,—with a glance or two in your direction,—he marches up behind the bench of the poor culprit,—who turns deathly pale,—grapples him by the collar, drags him out over the desks, his limbs dangling in a shocking way against the sharp angles, and having him fairly in the middle of the room, clinches his rod with a new, and, as it seems to you, a very sportive grip.

You shudder fearfully.

"Please don't whip me," says the boy whimpering.

"Aha!" says the smirking pedagogue, bringing down the stick with a quick, sharp cut,—"you don't like it, eh?"

The poor fellow screams, and struggles to escape; but the blows come faster and thicker. The blood tingles in your finger ends with indignation.

"Please don't strike me again," says the boy, sobbing and taking breath, as he writhes about the legs of the master;—"I won't read another time."

"Ah, you won't, sir—won't you? I don't mean you shall, sir," and the blows fall thick and fast,—until the poor fellow crawls back, utterly crest fallen and heart-sick, to sob over his books.

You grow into a sudden boldness: you wish you were only large enough to beat the master: you know such treatment would make you miserable: you shudder at the thought of it: you do not believe he would dare : you know the other boy has got no father. This seems to throw a new light upon the matter, but it only intensifies your indignation. You are sure that no father would suffer it; or if you thought so, it would sadly weaken your love for him. You pray Heaven that it may never be brought to such proof.

——Let a boy once distrust the love or the tenderness of his parents, and the last resort of his yearning affections—so far as the world goes—is utterly gone. He is in the sure road to a bitter fate. His heart will take on a hard iron covering, that will flash out plenty of fire in his after contact with the world, but it will never—never melt!

There are some tall trees that overshadow an angle of the school-house ; and the larger scholars play some very surprising gymnastic tricks upon their lower limbs : one boy, for instance, will hang for an incredible length of time by his feet, with his head down ; and when you tell Charlie of it at night, with such additions as your boyish imagination can contrive, the old nurse is shocked, and states very gravely that it is dangerous ; and that the blood all runs to the head, and sometimes bursts out of the eyes and mouth. You look at that particular boy with astonishment afterward; and expect to see him some day burst into bleeding from the nose and ears, and flood the school-room benches.

In time, however, you get to performing some modest experiments yourself upon the very lowest limbs,—taking care to avoid the observation of the larger boys, who else might laugh at you: you especially avoid the notice of one stout fellow in pea-green breeches, who is a sort of " bully " among the small boys, and who delights in kicking your marbles about, very accidentally. He has a fashion too of twisting his handkerchief into what he calls a " snapper," with a knot at the end, and cracking at you with it, very much to the irritation of your spirits, and of your legs.

Sometimes, when he has brought you to an angry burst of tears, he will very graciously force upon you the handkerchief, and insist upon your cracking him in return; which, as you know nothing about his effective method of making the knot bite, is a very harmless proposal on his part.

But you have still stronger reason to remember that boy. There are trees, as I said, near the school; and you get the reputation after a time of a good climber. One day you are well in the tops of the trees, and being dared by the boys below you venture higher—higher than any boy has ever gone before. You feel very proudly; but just then catch sight of the sneering face of your old enemy of the snapper; and he dares you to go upon a limb that he points out.

The rest say,—for you hear them plainly—" it won't bear him." And Frank, a great friend of yours, shouts loudly to you,—not to try.

" Pho," says your tormentor,—" the little coward!'

If you could whip him, you would go down the tree and do it willingly: as it is, you cannot let him triumph: so you advance cautiously out upon the limb: it bends and sways fearfully with your weight: presently it cracks: you try to return, but it is too late: you feel yourself going:—your mind flashes home—over your life—your hope—your fate, like lightning: then comes a sense of dizziness,—a succession of quick blows, and a dull, heavy crash!

You are conscious of nothing again, until you find yourself in the great hall of the school, covered with blood, the old Doctor standing over you with a phial, and Frank kneeling by you, and holding your shattered arm, which has been broken by the fall.

After this, come those long, weary days of confinement, when you lie still, through all the hours of noon, looking out upon the cheerful sunshine, only through the windows of your little room. Yet it seems a grand thing to have the whole household attendant upon you. The doors are opened and shut softly, and they all step noiselessly about your chamber; and when you groan with pain, you are sure of meeting sad, sympathizing looks. Your mother will step gently to your side and lay her cool, white hand upon your forehead; and little Nelly will gaze at you from the foot of your bed with a sad earnestness, and with tears of pity in her soft hazel eyes. And afterward, as your pain passes away, she will bring you her prettiest books, and fresh flowers, and whatever she knows you will love.

But it is dreadful, when you wake at night, from your feverish slumber, and see nothing but the spectral shadows that the sick-lamp upon the hearth throws aslant the walls; and hear nothing but the heavy breathing of the old nurse in the easy chair, and the ticking of the clock upon the mantel! Then, silence and the night crowd upon your soul drearily. But your thought is active. It shapes at your bed-side the loved figure of your mother, or it calls up the whole company of Dr. Bidlow's boys; and weeks of study or of play, group like magic on your quickened vision:—then, a twinge of pain will call again the dreariness, and your head tosses upon the pillow, and your eye searches the gloom vainly for pleasant faces; and your fears brood on that drearier, coming night of Death—far longer, and far more cheerless than this.

But even here, the memory of some little prayer you have been taught, which promises a Morning after the Night, comes to your throbbing brain; and its murmur on your fevered lips, as you breathe it, soothes like a caress of angels, and wooes you to smiles and sleep.

As the days pass, you grow stronger; and Frank comes in to tell you of the school, and that your old tormentor has been expelled: and you grow into a strong friendship with Frank, and you think of yourselves as a new Damon and Pythias—and that you will some day live together in a fine house, with plenty of horses, and plenty of chestnut trees. Alas, the boy counts little on those later and bitter fates of life, which sever his early friendships, like wisps of straw!

At other times, with your eye upon the sleek, trim figure of the Doctor, and upon his huge bunch of watch seals, you think you will some day be a Doctor; and that with a wife and children, and a respectable gig, and gold watch, with seals to match, you would needs be a very happy fellow.

And with such fancies drifting on your thought, you count for the hundredth time the figures upon the curtains of your bed, -you trace out the flower wreaths upon the paper-hangings of your room;— your eyes rest idly on the cat playing with the fringe of the curtain;—you see your mother sitting with her needle-work beside the fire;—you watch the sun-beams as they drift along the carpet, from morning until noon; and from noon till night, you watch them playing on the leaves, and dropping spangles on the lawn; and as you watch—you dream.

III.

Boy Sentiment.

WEEKS, and even years of your boyhood roll on, in the which your dreams are growing wider and grander,—even as the Spring, which I have made the type of the boy-age, is stretching its foliage farther and farther, and dropping longer and heavier shadows on the land.

Nelly, that sweet sister, has grown into your heart strangely; and you think that all they write in their books about love, cannot equal your fondness for little Nelly. She is pretty, they say; but what do you care for her prettiness? She is so good, so kind—so watchful of all your wants, so willing to yield to your haughty claims!

But, alas, it is only when this sisterly love is lost forever,—only when the inexorable world separates a family and tosses it upon the waves of fate to wide-lying distances—perhaps to graves!—that a man feels, what a boy can never know,—the disinterested and abiding affection of a sister.

All this, that I have set down, comes back to you long afterward, when you recall with tears of regret, your reproachful words or some swift outbreak of passion.

Little Madge is a friend of Nelly's—a mischievous, blue-eyed hoyden. They tease you about Madge. You do not of course care one straw for her, but yet it is rather pleasant to be teased thus. Nelly never does this; oh no, not she. I do not know but in the age of childhood, the sister is jealous of the affections of a brother, and would keep his heart wholly at home, until suddenly, and strangely, she finds her own—wandering.

But after all, Madge is pretty; and there is something taking in her name. Old people, and very precise people, call her Margaret Boyne. But you do not: it is only plain Madge;—it sounds like her—very rapid and mischievous. It would be the most absurd thing in the world for you to like her, for she teases you in innumerable ways: she laughs at your big shoes; (such a sweet little foot as she has!) and she pins strips of paper on your coat collar; and time and again she has borne off your hat in triumph, very well knowing that you, such a quiet body, and so much afraid of her, will never venture upon any liberties with her gipsy bonnet.

You sometimes wish, in your vexation, as you see her running, that she would fall and hurt herself badly; but the next moment, it seems a very wicked wish, and you renounce it. Once, she did come very near it. You were all playing together by the big swing—(how plainly it swings in your memory now!)—Madge had the seat, and you were famous for running under with a long push, which Madge liked better than anything else: well, you have half run over the ground, when crash comes the swing, and poor Madge with it! You fairly scream as you catch her up. But she is not hurt—only a cry of fright, and a little sprain of that fairy anlke; and as she brushes away the tears, and those flaxen curls, and breaks into a merry laugh,—half at your woe-worn face, and half in vexation at herself; and leans her hand (such a hand!) upon your shoulder, to limp away into the shade, you dream—your first dream of love.

But it is only a dream, not at all acknowledged by you: she is three or four years your junior,—too young altogether. It is very absurd to talk about it. There is nothing to be said of Madge—only—Madge! The name does it.

It is rather a pretty name to write. You are fond of making capital M's; and sometimes you follow it with a capital A. Then you practise a little upon a D, and perhaps back it up with a G. Of course it is the merest accident that these letters come together. It seems funny to you—very. And as a proof that they are made at random, you make a T or an R before them, and some other quite irrelevant letters after it.

Finally, as a sort of security against all suspicion, you cross it out—cross it a great many ways—even holding it up to the light, to see that there should be no air of intention about it.

——You need have no fear, Clarence, that your hieroglyphics will be studied so closely. Accidental as they are, you are very much more interested in them than any one else!

——It is a common fallacy of this dream in most stages of life, that a vast number of persons employ their time chiefly in spying out its operations.

Yet Madge cares nothing about you, that you know of. Perhaps it is the very reason, though you do not suspect it then, why you care so much for her. At any rate, she is a friend of Nelly's; and it is your duty not to dislike her. Nelly too, sweet Nelly, gets an inkling of matters; for sisters are very shrewd in suspicions of this sort—shrewder than brothers or fathers; and like the good kind girl that she is, she wishes to humor even your weakness.

Madge drops in to tea quite often: Nelly has something *in particular* to show her, two or three times a week. Good Nelly,—perhaps she is making your troubles all the greater! You gather large bunches of grapes for Madge—because she is a friend of Nelly's—which she doesn't want at all, and very pretty bouquets, which she either drops, or pulls to pieces.

In the presence of your father one day, you drop some hint about Madge, in a very careless way —a way shrewdly calculated to lay all suspicion;

—at which your father laughs. This is odd: it makes you wonder if your father was ever in love himself.

You rather think he has been.

Madge's father is dead and her mother is poor and you sometimes dream, how—whatever your father may think or feel—you will some day make a large fortune, in some very easy way, and build a snug cottage, and have one horse for your carriage, and one for your wife (not Madge, of course —that is absurd), and a turtle shell cat for your wife's mother, and a pretty gate to the front yard, and plenty of shrubbery, and how your wife will come dancing down the path to meet you,—as the Wife does in Mr. Irving's Sketch Book,—and how she will have a harp inside, and will wear white dresses, with a blue sash.

Poor Clarence, it never once occurs to you, that even Madge may grow fat, and wear check aprons, and snuffy-brown dresses of woollen stuff, and twist her hair in yellow papers! Oh no, boyhood has no such dreams as that!

I shall leave you here in the middle of your first foray into the world of sentiment, with those wicked blue eyes chasing rainbows over your heart, and those little feet walking every day into your affections. I shall leave you before the affair has ripened into any overtures, and while there is only a sixpence split in halves, and tied about your neck, and Maggie's neck, to bind your destinies together.

If I even hinted at any probability of your marrying her, or of your not marrying her, you would be very likely to dispute me. One knows his own feelings, or thinks he does, so much better than any one can tell him!

IV.

A Friend made and Friend Lost.

TO visit, is a great thing in the boy calendar:—not to visit this or that neighbor,—to drink tea, or eat strawberries, or play at draughts;—but, to go away on a visit in a coach, with a trunk, and a great-coat, and an umbrella:—this is large!

It makes no difference, that they wish to be rid of your noise, nor that Charlie is sick of a fever:—the reason is not at all in the way of your pride of visiting. You are to have a long ride in a coach, and eat a dinner at a tavern, and to see a new town almost as large as the one you live in and you are to make new acquaintances. In short, you are to see the world:—a very proud thing it is, to see the world!

As you journey on, after bidding your friends adieu, and as you see fences and houses to which you have not been used, you think them very odd indeed: but it occurs to you, that the geographies speak of very various national characteristics, and you are greatly gratified with this opportunity of verifying your study. You see new crops too, perhaps a broad-leaved tobacco field, which reminds you pleasantly of the luxuriant vegetation of the tropics, spoken of by Peter Parley, and others.

As for the houses and barns in the new town, they quite startle you with their strangeness: you observe that some of the latter instead of having one stable door, have five or six, a fact which puzzles you very much indeed. You observe farther, that the houses many of them have balustrades upon the top, which seems to you a very wonderful adaptation to the wants of boys, who wish to fly kites, or to play upon the roof. You notice with special favor, one very low roof which you might climb upon by a mere plank, and you think the boys, whose father lives in that house, are very fortunate boys.

Your old aunt, whom you visit, you think wears a very queer cap, being altogether different from that of the old nurse, or of Mrs. Boyne,—Madge's mother. As for the house she lives in, it is quite wonderful. There are such an immense number of closets, and closets within closets, reminding you of the mysteries of Rinaldo Rinaldini. Beside which, there are immensely curious bits of old furniture—so black and heavy, and with such curious carving!—and you think of the old wainscot in the Children of the Abbey. You think you will never tire of rambling about in its odd corners,

A FRIEND MADE AND FRIEND LOST. 63

and of what glorious stories you will have to tell of it, when you go back to Nelly, and Charlie.

As for acquaintances, you fall in the very first day with a tall boy next door, called Nat. which seems an extraordinary name. Besides, he has travelled; and as he sits with you on the summer nights under the linden trees, he tells you gorgeous stories of the things he has seen. He has made a voyage to London; and he talks about the ship (a real ship) and starboard and larboard, and the spanker, in a way quite surprising; and he takes the stern oar, in the little skiff when you row off in the cove abreast of the town, in a most seamanlike way.

He bewilders you too, with his talk about the great bridges of London—London Bridge specially, where they sell kids for a penny; which story your new acquaintance, unfortunately, does not confirm. You have read of these bridges, and seen pictures of them in the Wonders of the World; but then Nat. has seen them with his own eyes: he has literally walked over London Bridge on his own feet! You look at his very shoes in wonderment and are surprised you do not find some startling difference between those shoes, and your shoes. But there is none—only yours are a trifle stouter in the welt. You think Nat. one of the fortunate boys of this world—born, as your old nurse used to say—with a gold spoon in his mouth.

Beside Nat. there is a girl lives over the opposite side of the way, named Jenny, with an eye as black as a coal; and a half a year older than you; but about your height;—whom you fancy amazingly.

She has any quantity of toys, that she lets you play with, as if they were your own. And she has an odd, old uncle, who sometimes makes you stand up together, and then marries you after his fashion, —much to the amusement of a grown up house-maid, whenever she gets a peep at the performance. And it makes you somewhat proud to hear her called your wife; and you wonder to yourself, dreamily, if it won't be true some day or other.

———Fie, Clarence, where is your split sixpence, and your blue ribbon!

Jenny is romantic, and talks of Thaddeus of Warsaw in a very touching manner, and promises to lend you the book. She folds billets in a lover's fashion, and practises love-knots upon her bonnet strings. She looks out of the corners of her eyes very often, and sighs. She is frequently by herself, and pulls flowers to pieces. She has great pity for middle-aged bachelors, and thinks them all disappointed men.

After a time she writes notes to you, begging you would answer them at the earliest possible moment, and signs herself—'your attached Jenny.' She takes the marriage farce of her uncle in a cold way—as trifling with a very serious subject, and looks tenderly at you. She is very much shocked when her uncle offers to kiss her; and when he proposes it to you, she is equally indignant, but— with a great change of color.

Nat. says one day, in a confidential conversation, that it won't do to marry a woman six months older than yourself; and this coming from Nat. who has been to London, rather staggers you. You sometimes think that you would like to marry Madge and Jenny both, if the thing were possible; for Nat. says they sometimes do so the other side of the ocean, though he has never seen it himself.

——Ah, Clarence, you will have no such weakness as you grow older: you will find that Providence has charitably so tempered our affections, that every man of only ordinary nerve will be amply satisfied with a single wife!

All this time,—for you are making your visit a very long one, so that autumn has come, and the nights are growing cool, and Jenny and yourself are transferring your little coquetries to the chimney corner;—poor Charlie lies sick, at home. Boyhood, thank Heaven, does not suffer severely from sympathy when the object is remote. And those letters from the mother, telling you that Charlie cannot play,—cannot talk even as he used to do; and that perhaps his 'Heavenly Father will take him away, to be with him in the better world,' disturb you for a time only. Sometimes, however, they come back to your thoughts on a wakeful night, and you dream about his suffering, and think—why it is not you, but Charlie, who is sick? The thought puzzles you; and well it may, for in it lies the whole mystery of our fate.

Those letters grow more and more discouraging,

and the kind admonitions of your mother grow more earnest, as if (though the thought does not come to you until years afterward) she was preparing herself to fasten upon you that surplus of affection, which she fears may soon be withdrawn forever from the sick child.

It is on a frosty, bleak evening, when you are playing with Nat. that the letter reaches you which says Charlie is growing worse, and that you must come to your home. It makes a dreamy night for you—fancying how Charlie will look, and if sickness has altered him much, and if he will not be well by Christmas. From this, you fall away in your reverie, to the odd old house, and its secret cupboards, and your aunt's queer caps· then come up those black eyes of 'your attached Jenny,' and you think it a pity that she is six months older than you; and again—as you recal one of her sighs—you think—that six months are not much after all!

You bid her good-bye, with a little sentiment swelling in your throat, and are mortally afraid Nat. will see your lip tremble. Of course you promise to write, and squeeze her hand with an honesty you do not think of doubting—for weeks.

It is a dull, cold ride, that day, for you. The winds sweep over the withered corn-fields, with a harsh, chilly whistle; and the surfaces of the little pools by the road-side are tossed up into cold blue wrinkles of water. Here and there a flock of quail, with their feathers ruffled in the autumn gusts, tread through the hard, dry stubble of an oat-field; or startled by the snap of the driver's whip, they stare a moment at the coach, then whir away down the cold current of the wind. The blue jays scream from the road-side oaks, and the last of the blue and purple asters shiver along the wall. And as the sun sinks, reddening all the western clouds, to the color of the frosted maples,—light lines of the Aurora gush up from the northern hills, and trail their splintered fingers far over the autumn sky.

It is quite dark when you reach home, but you see the bright reflection of a fire within, and presently at the open door, Nelly clapping her hands for welcome. But there are sad faces when you enter. Your mother folds you to her heart; but at your first noisy out-burst of joy, puts her finger on her lip, and whispers poor Charlie's name. The Doctor you see too, slipping softly out of the bed-room door with glasses in his hand; and—you hardly know how—your spirits grow sad, and your heart gravitates to the heavy air of all about you.

You cannot see Charlie, Nelly says;—and you cannot in the quiet parlor, tell Nelly a single one of the many things, which you had hoped to tell her. She says—' Charlie has grown so thin and so pale, you would never know him.' You listen to her, but you cannot talk: she asks you what you have seen, and you begin, for a moment joyously; but when they open the door of the sick room, and you hear a faint sigh, you cannot go on. You sit still, with your hand in Nelly's, and look thoughtfully into the blaze.

You drop to sleep after that day's fatigue, with singular and perplexed fancies haunting you; and when you wake up with a shudder in the middle of the night, you have a fancy that Charlie is really dead: you dream of seeing him pale and thin, as Nelly described him, and with the starched grave clothes on him. You toss over your bed, and you grow hot and feverish. You cannot sleep; and you get up stealthily, and creep down stairs; a light is burning in the hall: the bed-room door stands half open, and you listen—fancying you hear a whisper. You steal on through the hall, and edge around the side of the door. A little lamp is flickering on the hearth, and the gaunt shadow of the bedstead lies dark upon the ceiling. Your mother is in her chair, with her head upon her hand—though it is long after midnight. The Doctor is standing with his back toward you, and with Charlie's little wrist in his fingers; and you hear hard breathing, and now and then, a low sigh from your mother's chair.

An occasional gleam of fire-light makes the gaunt shadow stagger on the wall, like something spectral. You look wildly at them, and then at the bed where your own brother—your laughing, gay-hearted brother, is lying. You long to see him, and slide up softly a step or two: but your mother's ear has caught the sound, and she beckons you to her, and folds you again in her

A FRIEND MADE AND FRIEND LOST. 69

embrace. You whisper to her what you wish. She rises, and takes you by the hand, to lead you to the bedside.

The Doctor looks very solemnly, as we approach. He takes out his watch. He is not counting Charlie's pulse, for he has dropped his hand; and it lies carelessly, but oh, how thin, over the edge of the bed.

He shakes his head mournfully at your mother; and she springs forward, dropping your hand, and lays her fingers upon the forehead of the boy, and passes her hand over his mouth.

"Is he asleep, Doctor?" she says, in a tone you do not know.

"Be calm, madam." The Doctor is very calm.

"I am calm," says your mother; but you do not think it, for you see her tremble very plainly.

"Dear madam, he will never waken in this world!"

There is no cry,—only a bowing down of your mother's head upon the body of poor, dead Charlie!—and only when you see her form shake and quiver with the deep, smothered sobs, your crying bursts forth loud and strong.

The Doctor lifts you in his arms, that you may see—that pale head,—those blue eyes all sunken,—that flaxen hair gone,—those white lips pinched and hard!——Never, never, will the boy forget his first terrible sight of Death!

In your silent chamber, after the storm of sobs

has wearied you, the boy-dreams are strange and earnest. They take hold on that awful Visitant,—that strange slipping away from life, of which we know so little, and yet know, alas, so much! Charlie that was your brother, is now only a name: perhaps he is an angel: perhaps (for the old nurse has said it, when he was ugly—and now, you hate her for it) he is with Satan.

But you are sure this cannot be: you are sure that God who made him suffer, would not now quicken, and multiply his suffering. It agrees with your religion to think so; and just now, you want your religion to help you all it can.

You toss in your bed, thinking over and over of that strange thing——Death:—and that perhaps it may overtake you, before you are a man; and you sob out those prayers (you scarce know why) which ask God to keep life in you. You think the involuntary fear that makes your little prayer full of sobs, is a holy feeling:—and so it is a holy feeling—the same feeling which makes a stricken child yearn for the embrace, and the protection of a Parent. But you will find there are those canting ones, trying to persuade you at a later day, that it is a mere animal fear, and not to be cherished.

You feel an access of goodness growing out of your boyish grief: you feel right-minded: it seems as if your little brother, in going to Heaven, had opened a pathway thither, down which, goodness comes streaming over your soul.

You think how good a life you will lead; and

you map out great purposes, spreading themselves over the school-weeks of your remaining boyhood; and you love your friends, or seem to, far more dearly than you ever loved them before; and you forgive the boy who provoked you to that sad fall from the oaks, and you forgive him all his wearisome teasings. But you cannot forgive yourself for some harsh words that you have once spoken to Charlie: still less can you forgive yourself for having once struck him, in passion, with your fist. You cannot forget his sobs then:——if he were only alive one little instant, to let you say,— "Charlie, will you forgive me?"

Yourself, you cannot forgive; and sobbing over it, and murmuring "Dear—dear Charlie!" -you drop into a troubled sleep.

V.

Boy Religion

IS any weak soul frightened, that I should write of the Religion of the boy? How indeed could I cover the field of his moral, or intellectual growth, if I left unnoticed those dreams of futurity and of goodness, which come sometimes to his quieter moments, and oftener, to his hours of vexation and trouble? It would be as wise to describe the season of Spring, with no note of the silent influences of that burning Day-god, which is melting day by day the shattered ice-drifts of Winter;—which is filling every bud with succulence, and painting one flower with crimson, and another with white.

I know there is a feeling—by much too general as it seems to me,—that the subject may not be approached, except through the dicta of certain ecclesiastic bodies;—and that the language which touches it, must not be that every-day language which mirrors the vitality of our thought,—but should have some twist of that theologic mannerism, which is as cold to the boy, as to the busy man of the world.

I know very well that a great many good souls will call levity, what I call honesty; and will abjure that familiar handling of the boy's lien upon Eternity, which my story will show. But I shall feel sure that in keeping true to Nature with word and with thought, I shall in no way offend against those Highest truths, to which all truthfulness is kindred.

You have Christian teachers, who speak always reverently of the Bible: you grow up in the hearing of daily prayers: nay, you are perhaps taught to say them.

Sometimes they have a meaning, and sometimes they have none. They have a meaning, when your heart is troubled,—when a grief or a wrong weighs upon you: then, the keeping of the Father, which you implore, seems to come from the bottom of your soul; and your eye suffuses with such tears of feeling, as you count holy, and as you love to cherish in your memory.

But they have no meaning, when some trifling vexation angers you, and a distaste for all about you, breeds a distaste for all above you. In the long hours of toilsome days, little thought comes over you of the morning prayer; and only when evening deepens its shadows, and your boyish vexations fatigue you to thoughtfulness, do you dream of that coming, and endless night, to which, —they tell you,—prayers soften the way.

Sometimes upon a Summer Sunday, when you are wakeful upon your seat in church, with some strong-worded preacher, who says things that half fright you, it occurs to you to consider how much goodness you are made of; and whether there be enough of it after all, to carry you safely away from the clutch of Evil? And straightway you reckon up those friendships where your heart lies: you know you are a true and honest friend to Frank; and you love your mother, and your father: as for Nelly, Heaven knows, you could not contrive a way to love her better than you do.

You dare not take much credit to yourself for the love of little Madge:—partly because you have sometimes caught yourself trying—not to love her: and partly because the black-eyed Jenny comes in the way. Yet you can find no command in the Catechism, to love one girl to the exclusion of all other girls. It is somewhat doubtful if you ever do find it. But, as for loving some half dozen you could name, whose images drift through your thought, in dirty, salmon-colored frocks, and slovenly shoes, it is quite impossible; and suddenly this thought, coupled with a lingering remembrance of the pea-green pantaloons, utterly breaks down your hopes.

Yet, you muse again,—there are plenty of good people as the times go, who have their dislikes, and who speak them too. Even the sharp-talking clergyman, you have heard say some very soul things about his landlord, who raised his rent the last year. And you know that he did not talk as mildly as he does in the Church, when he found Frank and yourself quietly filching a few of his peaches, through the orchard fence.

But your clergyman will say perhaps, with what seems to you, quite unnecessary coldness, that goodness is not to be reckoned in your chances of safety; —that there is a Higher Goodness, whose merit is All-Sufficient. This puzzles you sadly; nor will you escape the puzzle, until in the presence of the Home altar, which seems to guard you, as the Lares guarded Roman children, you *feel*—you cannot tell how,—that good actions must spring from good sources; and that those sources must lie in that Heaven, toward which your boyish spirit yearns, as you kneel at your mother's side.

Conscience too, is all the while approving you for deeds well done; and,—wicked as you fear the preacher might judge it,—you cannot but found on those deeds, a hope that your prayer at night flows more easily, more freely, and more holily toward "Our Father in Heaven." Nor indeed, later in life,—whatever may be the ill-advised expressions of human teachers,—will you ever find that *Duty performed*, and *generous endeavor* will stand one whit in the way either of Faith, or of Love. Striving to be good, is a very direct road toward Goodness; and if life be so tempered by high motive as to make actions always good, Faith is unconsciously won.

Another notion that disturbs you very much, is your positive dislike of long sermons, and of such singing as they have when the organist is away. You cannot get the force of that verse of Dr. Watts which likens heaven to a never-ending Sabbath; you *do* hope—though it seems a half wicked hope— that old Dr. —— will not be the preacher. You think that your heart in its best moments, craves for something more lovable. You suggest this perhaps to some Sunday teacher, who only shakes his head sourly, and tells you it is a thought that the Devil is putting in your brain. It strikes you oddly that the Devil should be using a verse of Dr. Watts to puzzle you! But if it be so, he keeps it sticking by your thought very pertinaciously, until some simple utterance of your mother about the Love that reigns in the other world, seems on a sudden to widen Heaven, and to waft away your doubts like a cloud.

It excites your wonder not a little, to find people who talk gravely and heartily of the excellence of sermons and of Church-going, do sometimes fall asleep under it all. And you wonder—if they really like preaching so well,—why they do not buy some of the minister's old manuscripts, and read them over on week-days;—or, invite the Clergyman to preach to them in a quiet way in private?

——Ah, Clarence, you do not yet know the poor weakness of even maturest manhood, and the feeble gropings of the soul toward a soul's paradise, in the best of the world! You do not yet know either that ignorance and fear will be thrusting their untruth and false show into the very essentials of Religion.

Again, you wonder,—if the Clergymen are all such very good men as you are taught to believe, why it is, that every little while people will be trying to send them off; and very anxious to prove that instead of being so good, they are in fact, very stupid and bad men. At that day, you have no clear conceptions of the distinction between stupidity and vice; and think that a good man must necessarily say very eloquent things. You will find yourself sadly mistaken on this point, before you get on very far in life.

Heaven, when your mother peoples it with friends gone, and little Charlie, and that better Friend, who, she says, took Charlie in his arms, and is now his Father, above the skies, seems a place to be loved, and longed for. But—to think that Mr. Such-an-one, who is only good on Sundays, will be there too; and to think of his talking as he does, of a place which you are sure he would spoil if he were there,—puzzles you again; and you relapse into wonder, doubt and yearning.

——And there, Clarence, for the present I shall leave you. A wide, rich Heaven hangs above you, but it hangs very high A wide, rough world is around you, and it lies very low!

I am assuming in these sketches no office of a teacher. I am seeking only to make a truthful analysis of the boyish thought and feeling. But having ventured thus far into what may seem sacred ground, I shall venture still farther, and clinch my matter with a moral.

There is very much Religious teaching, even in so good a country as New England, which is far too harsh, too dry, too cold for the heart of a boy. Long sermons, doctrinal precepts, and such tediously-worded dogmas as were uttered by these honest, but hard-spoken men—the Westminster Divines, fatigue, and puzzle, and dispirit him.

They may be well enough for those strong souls which strengthen by task-work, or for those mature people whose iron habit of self-denial has made patience a cardinal virtue; but they fall (*experto crede*) upon the unfledged faculties of the boy, like a winter's rain upon Spring flowers,—like hammers of iron upon lithe timber. They may make deep impression upon his moral nature, but there is great danger of a sad rebound.

Is it absurd to suppose that some adaptation is desirable? And might not the teachings of that Religion, which is the Ægis of our moral being, be inwrought with some of those finer harmonies of speech and form—which were given to wise ends; —and lure the boyish soul, by something akin to that gentleness, which belonged to the Nazarene Teacher; and which provided—not only, meat for men, but "milk for babes?"

VI.

A New England Squire.

FRANK has a grandfather living in the country, a good specimen of the old fashioned New England farmer. And—go where one will, the world over—I know of no race of men, who taken together, possess more integrity, more intelligence, and more of those elements of comfort, which go to make a home beloved, and the social basis firm, than the New England farmers.

They are not brilliant, nor are they highly refined; they know nothing of arts, histrionic or dramatic; they know only so much of older nations as their histories and newspapers teach them; in the fashionable world they hold no place;—but in energy, in industry, in hardy virtue, in substantial knowledge, and in manly independence, they make up a race, that is hard to be matched.

The French peasantry are, in all the essentials of intelligence, and sterling worth, infants, compared with them: and the farmers of England are either the merest jockies in grain, with few ideas beyond their sacks, samples, and market-days;—or with added cultivation, they lose their independence in a subserviency to some neighbor patron of rank, and superior intelligence teaches them no lesson so quickly, as that their brethren of the glebe are unequal to them, and are to be left to their cattle and the goad.

There are English farmers indeed, who are men in earnest, who read the papers, and who keep the current of the year's intelligence; but such men are the exceptions. In New England, with the school upon every third hill-side, and the self-regulating, free-acting church, to watch every valley with week-day quiet, and to wake every valley with Sabbath sound, the men become as a class, bold, intelligent, and honest actors, who would make again, as they have made before, a terrible army of defence; and who would find reasons for their actions, as strong as their armies.

Frank's grandfather has silver hair, but is still hale, erect, and strong. His dress is homely, but neat. Being a thorough-going Protectionist, he has no fancy for the gew-gaws of foreign importation, and makes it a point to appear always in the village church, and on all great occasions, in a sober suit of homespun. He has no pride of appearance, and he needs none. He is known as the Squire, throughout the township, and no important measure can pass the board of select-men without the Squire's approval:—and this, from no blind subserviency to his opinion, because his farm is large, and he is reckoned "fore-handed," but because there is a confidence in his judgment.

He is jealous of none of the prerogatives of the country parson, or of the school-master, or of the Village doctor; and although the latter is a testy politician of the opposite party, it does not at all impair the Squire's faith in his calomel;—he suffers all his Radicalism, with the same equanimity that he suffers his rhubarb.

The day-laborers of the neighborhood, and the small farmers consider the Squire's note of hand for their savings, better than the best bonds of city origin; and they seek his advice in all matters of litigation. He is a Justice of the Peace, as the title of Squire in a New England village implies; and many are the country courts that you peep upon, with Frank, from the door of the great dining room.

The defendant always seems to you, in these important cases,—especially if his beard is rather long,—an extraordinary ruffian; to whom Jack Sheppard would have been a comparatively innocent boy. You watch curiously the old gentleman, sitting in his big arm chair, with his spectacles in their silver case at his elbow, and his snuff box in hand, listening attentively to some grievous complaint; you see him ponder deeply—with a pinch of snuff to aid his judgment,—and you listen with intense admiration, as he gives a loud, preparatory "Ahem," and clears away the intricacies of the case with a sweep of that strong practical sense, which distinguishes the New England farmer,—getting at the very hinge of the matter, without any consciousness of his own precision, and satisfying the defendant by the clearness of his talk, as much as by the leniency of his judgment.

His lands lie along those swelling hills which in southern New England, carry the chain of the White and Green Mountains, in gentle undulations, to the borders of the sea. He farms some fifteen hundred acres,—"suitably divided," as the old school agriculturists say, into "wood-land, pasture, and tillage." The farm-house, a large irregularly built mansion of wood, stands upon a shelf of the hills southward, and is shaded by century-old oaks. The barns and out-buildings are grouped in a brown phalanx, a little to the northward of the dwelling. Between them a high timber gate, opens upon the scattered pasture lands of the hills: opposite to this, and across the farm-yard which is the lounging place of scores of red-necked turkeys, and of matronly hens, clucking to their callow brood, another gate of similar pretensions opens upon the wide meadow land, which rolls with a heavy "ground swell," along the valley of a mountain river. A veteran oak stands sentinel at the brown meadow-gate, its trunk all scarred with the ruthless cuts of new-ground axes, and the limbs garnished in summer time, with the crooked snathes of murderous-looking scythes.

The high-road passes a stone's throw away,

but there is little "travel" to be seen; and every chance passer will inevitably come under the range of the kitchen windows, and be studied carefully by the eyes of the stout dairy-maid :—to say nothing of the stalwart Indian cook.

This last, you cannot but admire as a type of that noble race, among whom your boyish fancy has woven so many stories of romance. You wonder how she must regard the white interlopers upon her own soil; and you think that she tolerates the Squire's farming privileges, with more modesty than you would suppose. You learn, however, that she pays very little regard to white rights,—when they conflict with her own; and further learn, to your deep regret, that your Princess of the old tribe is sadly addicted to cider drinking: and having heard her once or twice, with a very indistinct "Goo-er night Sq-quare," upon her lips—your dreams about her grow very lame.

The Squire, like all very sensible men, has his hobbies, and peculiarities. He has a great contempt, for instance, for all paper money; and imagines banks to be corporate societies, skilfully contrived for the legal plunder of the community. He keeps a supply of silver and gold by him, in the foot of an old stocking; and seems to have great confidence in the value of Spanish milled dollars. He has no kind of patience with the new doctrines of farming. Liebig, and all the rest, he sets down as mere theorists; and has far more respect for the contents of his barn-yard, than for all the guano deposits in the world. Scientific farming, and gentleman farming, may do very well, he says, 'to keep idle young fellows from the City out of mischief; but as for real, effective management, there's nothing like the old stock of men, who ran barefoot until they were ten, and who count the hard winters by their frozen toes.' And he is fond of quoting in this connection,—the only quotation by the by, that the old gentleman ever makes—that couplet of Poor Richard:—

> He that by the plough would thrive,
> Himself must either hold or drive.

The Squire has been in his day, connected more or less intimately with Turn-pike enterprise, which the rail-roads of the day have thrown sadly into the back-ground; and he reflects often, in a melancholy way, upon the good old times when a man could travel in his own carriage quietly across the country, without being frightened with the clatter of an engine;—and when Turn-pike stock paid wholesome yearly dividends of six per cent.

An almost constant hanger-on about the premises, and a great favorite with the Squire, is a stout, middle-aged man, with a heavy bearded face—to whom Frank introduces you, as "Captain Dick;" and he tells you moreover, that he is a better butcher,—a better wall layer, and cuts a broader "swathe," than any man upon the farm. Beside all which, he has an immense deal of information. He knows, 'n the Spring, where all the crows' nests are to be found; he tells Frank where the foxes burrow; he has even shot two or three raccoons in the swamps; he knows the best season to troll for pickerel; he has a thorough understanding of bee-hunting; he can tell the ownership of every stray heifer that appears upon the road: indeed, scarce an inquiry is made, or an opinion formed, on any of these subjects, or on such kindred ones as the weather, or potato crop, without previous consultation with "Captain Dick."

You have an extraordinary respect for Captain Dick: his gruff tones, dark beard, patched waistcoat, and cow-hide boots, only add to it: you can compare your regard for him, only with the sentiments you entertain for those fabulous Roman heroes, led on by Horatius, who cut down the bridge across the Tiber, and then swam over to their wives and families.

A superannuated old greyhound lives about the premises, and stalks lazily around, thrusting his thin nose into your hands, in a very affectionate manner.

Of course, in your way, you are a lion among the boys of the neighborhood: a blue jacket that you wear, with bell buttons of white metal, is their especial wonderment. You astonish them, moreover, with your stories of various parts of the world which they have never visited. They tell you of the haunts of rabbits, and great snake stories, as you sit in the dusk after supper, under the old oaks; and you delight them in turn, with some marvellous tale of South American reptiles, out of Peter Parley's books.

In all this, your new friends are men of observation; while Frank and yourself are comparatively men of reading. In ciphering, and all schooling, you find yourself a long way before them; and you talk of problems, and foreign seas, and Latin declensions, in a way that sets them all agape.

As for the little country girls, their bare legs rather stagger your notions of propriety; nor can you wholly get over their outside pronunciation of some of the vowels. Frank, however, has a little cousin,—a toddling, wee thing, some seven years your junior, who has a rich eye for an infant. But, alas, its color means nothing; poor Fanny is stone blind! Your pity leans toward her strangely, as she feels her way about the old parlor; and her dark eyes wander over the wainscot, or over the clear, blue sky—with the same, sad, painful vacancy.

And yet—it is very strange!—she does not grieve: there is a sweet, soft smile upon her lip,—a smile that will come to you in your fancied troubles of after life, with a deep voice of reproach.

Altogether, you grow into a liking of the country: your boyish spirit loves its fresh, bracing air, and the sparkles of dew, that at sunrise cover the hills with diamonds;—and the wild river, with its black-topped, loitering pools;—and the shaggy mists that lie, in the nights of early autumn, like unravelled clouds, lost upon the meadow. You love the hills climbing green and grand to the skies, or stretching away in distance, their soft, blue, smoky caps,—like the sweet, half-faded memories of the years behind you. You love those oaks tossing up their broad arms into clear heaven, with a spirit and a strength, that kindle your dawning pride and purposes; and that make you yearn, as your forehead mantles with fresh blood, for a kindred spirit, and a kindred strength. Above all, you love—though you do not know it now—the BREADTH of a country life. In the fields of God's planting, there is ROOM. No walls of brick and mortar cramp one: no factitious distinctions mould your habit. The involuntary reaches of the spirit, tend toward the True, and the Natural. The flowers, the clouds, and the fresh-smelling earth, all give width to your intent. The boy grows into manliness, instead of growing to be like men. He claims,—with tears almost, of brotherhood,—his kinship with Nature; and he feels, in the mountains, his heirship to the Father of Nature!

This delirium of feeling may not find expression upon the lip of the boy; but yet it underlies his thought, and will, without his consciousness, give the spring to his musing dreams.

——So it is, that as you lie there upon the sunny greensward, at the old Squire's door, you muse upon the time when some rich lying land, with huge granaries, and cozy old mansion sleeping under the trees, shall be yours;—when the brooks shall water your meadows, and come laughing down your pasture lands;—when the clouds shall shed their spring fragrance upon your lawns, and the daisies bless your paths.

You will then be a Squire, with your cane, your lean-limbed hound, your stocking-leg of specie, and your snuff-box. You will be the happy, and respected husband of some tidy old lady in black, and spectacles,—a little phthisicky, like Frank's grandmother,—an accomplished cook of stewed pears, and Johnny cakes!

It seems a very lofty ambition, at this stage of growth, to reach such eminence, as to convert your drawer in the wainscot, that has a secret spring, into a bank for the country people; and the power to send a man to jail, seems one of those stretches of human prerogative, to which few of your fellow mortals can ever hope to attain.

——Well, it may all be. And who knows but the Dreams of Age, when they are reached, will be lighted by the same spirit and freedom of nature that is around you now? Who knows, but that after tracking you through the Spring, and the Summer of Youth, we shall find frosted Age settling upon you heavily, and solemnly, in the very fields where you wanton to-day?

This American life of ours is a tortuous and shifting impulse. It brings Age back, from years of wandering, to totter in the hamlet of its birth· and it scatters armies of ripe manhood, to bleach far-away shores with their bones.

That Providence, whose eye and hand are the spy and the executioner of the Fateful changes of our life, may bring you back in Manhood, or in Age, to this mountain home of New England ; and that very willow yonder, which your fancy now makes the graceful mourner of your leave, may one day shadow mournfully your grave!

VII.

The Country Church.

THE country church is a square old building of wood, without paint or decoration—and of that genuine, Puritanic stamp, which is now fast giving way to Greek porticos, and to cockney towers. It stands upon a hill with a little church-yard in its rear, where one or two sickly looking trees keep watch and ward over the vagrant sheep that graze among the graves. Bramble bushes seem to thrive on the bodies below, and there is no flower in the little yard, save a few golden rods, which flaunt their gaudy inodorous color under the lee of the northern wall.

New England country-livers have as yet been very little inoculated with the sentiment of beauty; even the door-step to the church is a wide flat stone, that shows not a single stroke of the hammer. Within, the simplicity is even more severe. Brown galleries run around three sides of the old building, supported by timbers, on which you still trace, under the stains from the leaky roof, the deep scoring of the woodman's axe.

Below, the unpainted pews are ranged in square forms, and by age, have gained the color of those fragmentary wrecks of cigar boxes, which you see upon the top shelves, in the bar-rooms of country taverns. The minister's desk is lofty, and has once been honored with a coating of paint;—as well as the huge sounding-board, which, to your great amazement, protrudes from the wall, at a very dangerous angle of inclination, over the speaker's head. As the Squire's pew is the place of honor, to the right of the pulpit, you have a little tremor yourself, at sight of the heavy sounding-board, and cannot forbear indulging in a quiet feeling of relief when the last prayer is said.

There are in the Squire's pew, long, faded, crimson cushions; which, it seems to you, must date back nearly to the commencement of the Christian era in this country. There are also sundry old thumb-worn copies of Dr. Dwight's Version of the Psalms of David—'appointed to be sung in churches, by authority of the General Association of the State of Connecticut.' The sides of Dr. Dwight's Version are, you observe, sadly warped, and weather-stained; and from some stray figures which appear upon a fly-leaf, you are constrained to think, that the Squire has sometime employed a quiet interval of the service, with reckoning up the contents of the old stocking-leg at home.

The parson is a stout man, remarkable in your opinion, chiefly for a yellowish-brown wig, a strong nasal tone, and occasional violent thumps upon the little, dingy, red velvet cushion, studded with brass tacks, at the top of the desk. You do not altogether admire his style; and by the time he has entered upon his "Fourthly," you give your attention, in despair, to a new reading (it must be the twentieth) of the preface to Dr. Dwight's Version of the Psalms.

The singing has a charm for you. There is a long, thin-faced, flax-haired man, who carries a tuning fork in his waistcoat pocket, and who leads the choir. His position is in the very front rank of gallery benches, facing the desk; and by the time the old clergyman has read two verses of the psalm, the country chorister turns around to his little group of aids—consisting of the blacksmith, a carroty headed school-master, two women in snuff-colored silks, and a girl in pink bonnet—to announce the tune.

This being done in an authoritative manner, he lifts his long music book,—glances again at his little company,—clears his throat by a powerful ahem, followed by a powerful use of a bandanna pocket-handkerchief,—draws out his tuning fork, and waits for the parson to close his reading. He now reviews once more his company,—throws a reproving glance at the young woman in the pink hat, who at the moment is biting off a stout bunch of fennel —lifts his music book,—thumps upon the rail with his fork,—listens keenly,—gives a slight *ahem*,—falls into the cadence,—swells into a strong *crescendo*,—catches at the first word of the line, as if he were afraid it might get away,—turns to his company,—lifts his music book with spirit,—gives it a powerful slap with the disengaged hand, and with a majestic toss of the head, soars away, with half the women below straggling on in his wake, into some such brave, old melody as——LITCH-FIELD!

Being a visitor, and in the Squire's pew, you are naturally an object of considerable attention to the girls about your age; as well as to a great many fat, old ladies in iron spectacles, who mortify you excessively, by patting you under the chin after church; and insist upon mistaking you for Frank; and force upon you very dry cookies, spiced with caraway seeds.

You keep somewhat shy of the young ladies, as they are rather stout for your notions of beauty; and wear thick calf-skin boots. They compare very poorly with Jenny. Jenny, you think, would be above eating ginger-bread between service. None of them, you imagine, even read Thaddeus of Warsaw, or ever used a colored glass seal with a heart upon it. You are quite certain they never did, or they could not, surely, wear such dowdy gowns, and suck their thumbs as they do!

The farmers you have a high respect for;—particularly for one weazen-faced old gentleman in a brown surtout, who brings his whip into church with him, who sings in a very strong voice, and who drives a span of grey colts. You think, however, that he has got rather a stout wife; and from the way he humors her in stopping to talk with two or three other fat women, before setting off for home (though he seems a little fidgetty), you naïvely think, that he has a high regard for her opinion. Another townsman, who attracts your notice, is a stout old deacon, who before entering, always steps around the corner of the church, and puts his hat upon the ground, to adjust his wig in a quiet way. He then marches up the broad aisle in a stately manner, and plants his hat, and a big pair of buckskin mittens, on the little table under the desk. When he is fairly seated in his corner of the pew, with his elbow upon the top-rail—almost the only man who can comfortably reach it,—you observe that he spreads his brawny fingers over his scalp, in an exceedingly cautious manner; and you innocently think again, that it is very hypocritical in a Deacon, to be pretending to lean upon his hand, when he is only keeping his wig straight.

After the morning service, they have an 'hour's intermission,' as the preacher calls it; during which the old men gather on a sunny side of the building, and after shaking hands all around, and asking after the 'folks' at home, they enjoy a quiet talk about the crops. One man, for instance, with a twist in his nose, would say, 'it's raether a growin' season;' and another would reply—'tolerable, but potatoes is feelin' the wet, badly.' The stout deacon approves this opinion, and confirms it, by blowing his nose very powerfully.

Two or three of the more wordly minded ones, will perhaps stroll over to a neighbor's barn-yard, and take a look at his young stock, and talk of prices, and whittle a little; and very likely some two of them, will make a conditional 'swop' of 'three likely yer'lings' for a pair of 'two-year-olds.'

The youngsters are fond of getting out into the grave-yard, and comparing jack-knives, or talking about the school-master, or the menagerie;—or, it may be, of some prospective 'travel' in the fall,— either to town or perhaps to the 'sea-shore.'

Afternoon service hangs heavily; and the tall chorister is by no means so blithe, or so majestic in the toss of his head, as in the morning. A boy in the next box, tries to provoke you into familiarity by dropping pellets of gingerbread through the bars of the pew; but as you are not accustomed to that way of making acquaintance, you decline all overtures.

After the service is finished, the wagons that have been disposed on either side of the road, are drawn up before the door. The old Squire meantime, is sure to have a little chat with the parson before he leaves; in the course of which, the parson takes occasion to say that his wife is a little ailing —'a slight touch,' he thinks, 'of the rheumatiz.

One of the children too, has been troubled with the 'summer complaint' for a day or two; but he thinks that a dose of catnip, under Providence, will effect a cure. The younger, and unmarried men, with red wagons, flaming upon bright, yellow wheels, make great efforts to drive off in the van; and they spin frightfully near some of the fat, sour-faced women, who remark in a quiet, but not very Christian tone, that 'they fear the elder's sermon hasn't done the young bucks much good.' It is much to be feared, in truth, that it has not.

In ten minutes the old church is thoroughly deserted; the neighbor who keeps the key has locked up for another week, the creaking door; and nothing of the service remains within, except—Dr. Dwight's version,—the long music books,—crumbs of gingerbread, and refuse stalks of despoiled fennel.

And yet, under the influence of that old weather-stained temple, are perhaps growing up—though you do not once fancy it—souls, possessed of an energy, an industry, and a respect for virtue, which will make them stronger for the real work of life, than all the elegant children of a city. One lesson, which even the rudest churches of New England teach,—with all their harshness, and all their repulsive severity of form—is the lesson of SELF-DENIAL. Once armed with that, and manhood is strong. The soul that possesses the consciousness of mastering passion, is endowed with an element of force, that can never harmonize with defeat. Difficulties, it wears like a summer garment, and flings away, at the first approach of the winter of NEED.

Let not any one suppose then, that in this detail of the country life, through which our hero is led, I would cast obloquy, or a sneer, upon its simplicity, or upon its lack of refinement. Goodness, and strength, in this world, are quite as apt to wear rough coats, as fine ones. And the words of thorough, and self-sacrificing kindness, are far more often dressed in the uncouth sounds of retired life, than in the polished utterance of the town. Heaven has not made warm hearts, and honest hearts distinguishable by the quality of the covering. True diamonds need no work of the artificer to reflect, and multiply their rays. Goodness is more within, than without; and purity is of nearer kin to the soul, than to the body.

——And, Clarence, it may well happen, that later in life—under the gorgeous ceilings of Venetian churches, or at some splendid mass of Notre Dame, with embroidered coats, and costly silks around you,—your thoughts will run back to that little storm-beaten church, and to the willow waving in its yard—with a Hope that *glows*;—and with a tear, that you embalm!

VIII.

A Home Scene.

AND now I shall not leave this realm of boyhood, or suffer my hero to slip away from this gala time of his life, without a fair look at that Home where his present pleasures lie, and where all his dreams begin and end.

Little does the boy know, as the tide of years drifts by, floating him out insensibly from the harbor of his home, upon the great sea of life,—what joys, what opportunities, what affections, are slipping from him into the shades of that inexorable Past, where no man can go, save on the wings of his dreams. Little does he think—and God be praised, that the thought does not sink deep lines in his young forehead!—as he leans upon the lap of his mother, with his eye turned to her, in some earnest pleading for a fancied pleasure of the hour, or in some important story of his griefs, that such sharing of his sorrows, and such sympathy with his wishes, he will find no where again.

Little does he imagine, that the fond Nelly, ever thoughtful of his pleasures, ever smiling away his griefs—will soon be beyond the reach of either; and that the waves of the years which come rocking so gently under him will soon toss her far away, upon the great swell of life.

But *now*, you are there. The fire-light glimmers upon the walls of your cherished home, like the Vestal fire of old upon the figures of adoring virgins, or like the flame of Hebrew sacrifice, whose incense bore hearts to Heaven. The big chair of your father is drawn to its wonted corner by the chimney side; his head, just touched with gray, lies back upon its oaken top. Little Nelly leans upon his knee, looking up for some reply, to her girlish questionings. Opposite sits your mother; her figure is thin, her look cheerful, yet subdued;—her arm perhaps resting on your shoulder, as she talks to you in tones of tender admonition, of the days that are to come.

The cat is purring on the hearth; the clock that ticked so plainly when Charlie died, is ticking on the mantel still. The great table in the middle of the room, with its books and work, waits only for the lighting of the evening lamp, to see a return to its stores of embroidery, and of story.

Upon a little stand under the mirror, which catches now and then a flicker of the fire-light, and makes it play, as if in wanton, upon the ceiling, lies that big book, reverenced of your New England parents—the Family Bible. It is a ponderous square volume, with heavy silver clasps, that you have often pressed open for a look at its quaint old pictures, or for a study of those prettily bordered pages, which lie between the Testaments, and which hold the Family Record.

There are the Births;—your father's, and your mother's; it seems as if they were born a long time ago; and even your own date of birth appears an almost incredible distance back. Then, there are the marriages;—only one as yet; and your mother's maiden name looks oddly to you: it is hard to think of her as any one else than your doting parent. You wonder if your name will ever come under that paging; and wonder, though you scarce whisper the wonder to yourself, how another name would look, just below yours—such a name for instance, as Fanny,—or as Miss Margaret Boyne!

Last of all, come the Deaths—only one. Poor Charlie! How it looks?—' Died 12 September, 18— Charles Henry, aged four years.' You know just how it looks. You have turned to it often; there you seem to be joined to him, though only by the turning of a leaf. And over your thoughts, as you look at that page of the record, there sometimes wanders a vague shadowy fear, which *will* come,— that your own name may soon be there. You try to drop the notion, as if it were not fairly your own; you affect to slight it, as you would slight a boy who presumed on your acquaintance, but whom you have no desire to know. It is a common thing, you will find, with our world, to decline familiarity with those ideas that fright us.

Yet your mother—how strange it is!—has no

fears of such dark fancies. Even now, as you stand beside her, and as the twilight deepens in the room her low, silvery voice is stealing upon your ear telling you that she cannot be long with you;—that the time is coming, when you must be guided by your own judgment, and struggle with the world, un aided by the friends of your boyhood. There is a little pride, and a great deal more of anxiety in your thoughts now,—as you look steadfastly into the home blaze, while those delicate fingers so tender of your happiness, play with the locks upon your brow.

——To struggle with the world,—that is a proud thing; to struggle alone,--there lies the doubt! Then, crowds in swift, upon the calm of boyhood, the first anxious thought of youth;—then chases over the sky of Spring, the first heated, and wrathful cloud of Summer!

But the lamps are now lit in the little parlor, and they shed a soft haze to the farthest corner of the room; while the fire light streams over the floor where puss lies purring. Little Madge is there; she has dropped in softly with her mother, and Nelly has welcomed her with a bound, and with a kiss. Jenny has not so rosy a cheek as Madge. But Jenny with her love notes, and her languishing dark eye, you think of, as a lady; and the thought of her is a constant drain upon your sentiment. As for Madge—that girl Madge, whom you know so well,—you think of her as a sister, and yet—it is very odd,—you look at her far oftener than you do at Nelly!

5*

Frank too has come in to have a game with you at draughts; and he is in capital spirits, all brisk and glowing with his evening's walk. He,—bless his honest heart!—never observes that you arrange the board very adroitly, so that you may keep half an eye upon Madge, as she sits yonder beside Nelly. Nor does he once notice your blush, as you catch her eye, when she raises her head to fling back the ringlets; and then, with a sly look at you, bends a most earnest gaze upon the board, as if she were especially interested in the disposition of the men.

You catch a little of the spirit of coquetry yourself—(what a native growth it is!) and if she lift her eyes, when you are gazing at her, you very suddenly divert your look to the cat at her feet; and remark to your friend Frank, in an easy, off-hand way—how still the cat is lying!

And Frank turns—thinking probably, if he thinks at all about it, that cats are very apt to lie still, when they sleep.

As for Nelly, half neglected by your thought, as well as by your eye, while mischievous looking Madge is sitting by her, you little know as yet, what kindness—what gentleness, you are careless of. Few loves in life, and you will learn it before life is done, can balance the lost love of a sister.

As for your parents, in the intervals of the game you listen dreamily to their talk with the mother of Madge—good Mrs. Boyne. It floats over your mind, as you rest your chin upon your clenched hand, like a strain of old familiar music,—a household strain, that seems to belong to the habit of your ear,—a strain that will linger about it melodiously for many years to come,—a strain that will be recalled long time hence, when life is earnest and its cares heavy, with tears of regret, and with sighs of bitterness.

By and by your game is done; and other games, in which join Nelly (the tears come when you write her name, *now!*) and Madge (the smiles come when you look on her, *then*), stretch out that sweet eventide of Home, until the lamp flickers, and you speak your friends—adieu. To Madge, it is said boldly —a boldness put on to conceal a little lurking tremor;—but there is no tremor in the home goodnight.

——Aye, my boy, kiss your mother—kiss her again;—fondle your sweet Nelly;—pass your little hand through the gray locks of your father;—love them dearly, while you can! Make your goodnights linger; and make your adieus long, and sweet, and often repeated. Love with your whole soul,— Father, Mother, and Sister;—for these loves shall die!

——Not indeed in thought:—God be thanked! —Nor yet in tears,—for He is merciful! But they shall die as the leaves die,—die as Spring dies into the heat, and ripeness of Summer, and as boyhood dies into the elasticity and ambition of youth. Death, distance, and time, shall each one of them dig graves for your affections; but this you do not know, nor can know, until the story of your life is ended.

The dreams of riches, of love, of voyage, of learning, that light up the boy-age with splendor, will pass on and over into the hotter dreams of youth. Spring buds and blossoms under the glowing sun of April, nurture at their heart those firstlings of fruit, which the heat of summer shall ripen.

You little know,—and for this you may well thank Heaven—that you are leaving the Spring of life, and that you are floating fast from the shady sources of your years, into heat, bustle, and storm. Your dreams are now faint, flickering shadows, that play like fire-flies in the coppices of leafy June. They have no rule, but the rule of infantile desire. They have no joys to promise, greater than the joys that belong to your passing life; they have no terrors but such terrors as the darkness of a Spring night makes. They do not take hold on your soul, as the dreams of youth and manhood will do.

Your highest hope is shadowed in a cheerful, boyish home. You wish no friends but the friends of boyhood;—no sister but your fond Nelly;—none to love better than the playful Madge.

You forget, Clarence, that the Spring with you, is the Spring with them; and that the storms of Summer may chase wide shadows over your path, and over theirs. And you forget, that SUMMER is even now, lowering with its mist, and with its scorching rays, upon the hem of your flowery May!

———The hands of the old clock upon the mantel, that ticked off the hours when Charlie sighed, and when Charlie died, draw on toward midnight. The shadows that the fire-flame makes, grow dimmer and dimmer And thus it is, that Home, boy-home, passes away forever,—like the swaying of a pendulum,—like the fading of a shadow on the floor!

Summer;

OR,

THE DREAMS OF YOUTH.

DREAMS OF YOUTH.

Summer.

I FEEL a great deal of pity for those honest, but misguided people, who call their little, spruce suburban towns, or the shaded streets of their inland cities,—the country: and I have still more pity for those who reckon a season at the summer resorts—country enjoyment. Nay, my feeling is more violent than pity; and I count it nothing less than blasphemy, so to take the name of the country in vain.

I thank Heaven every summer's day of my life, that my lot was humbly cast, within the hearing of romping brooks, and beneath the shadow of oaks. And from all the tramp and bustle of the world, into which fortune has led me in these latter years of my life, I delight to steal away for days, and for weeks together, and bathe my spirit in the f.eedom of the old woods; and to grow young again, lying upon the brook side, and counting the white clouds that sail along the sky, softly and tranquilly—even as holy memories go stealing over the vault of life.

I am deeply thankful that I could never find it in my heart, so to pervert truth, as to call the smart villages with the tricksy shadow of their maple avenues—the Country.

I love these in their way; and can recall pleasant passages of thought, as I have idled through the Sabbath-looking towns, or lounged at the inn-door of some quiet New England village. But I love far better to leave them behind me and to dash boldly out to where some out-lying farm-house sits—like a witness—under shelter of wooded hills, or nestles in the lap of a noiseless valley.

In the town, small as it may be, and darkened as it may be with the shadows of trees, you cannot forget—men. Their voice, and strife, and ambition come to your eye in the painted paling, in the swinging sign-board of the tavern, and—worst of all—in the trim-printed "ATTORNEY AT LAW." Even the little milliner's shop, with its meagre show of leghorns, and its string across the window, all hung with tabs and with cloth roses, is a sad epitome of the great and conventional life of a city neighborhood.

I like to be rid of them all, as I am rid of them this mid-summer's day. I like to steep my soul in a sea of quiet, with nothing floating past me as I lie moored to my thought, but the perfume of flowers, and soaring birds, and shadows of clouds.

Two days since, I was sweltering in the heat of the City, jostled by the thousand eager workers, and panting under the shadow of the walls. But I have stolen away; and for two hours of healthful regrowth into the darling Past, I have been lying this blessed summer's morning, upon the grassy bank of a stream that babbled me to sleep in boyhood. ——Dear, old stream, unchanging, unfaltering,—with no harsher notes now than then,—never growing old,—smiling in your silver rustle, and calming yourself in the broad, placid pools,—I love you as I love a friend!

But now, that the sun has grown scalding hot, and the waves of heat have come rocking under the shadow of the meadow oaks, I have sought shelter in a chamber of the old farm-house. The window-blinds are closed; but some of them are sadly shattered, and I have intertwined in them a few branches of the late-blossoming, white Azalia, so that every puff of the summer air comes to me cooled with fragrance. A dimple or two of the sunlight still steals through my flowery screen, and dances (as the breeze moves the branches) on the oaken floor of the farm-house.

Through one little gap indeed, I can see the broad stretch of meadow, and the wor'-men in the field bending and swaying to their scythes. I can see too the glistening of the steel, as they wipe their blades; and can just catch floating on the air, the measured, tinkling thwack of the rifle stroke.

Here and there a lark, scared from his feeding

place in the grass, soars up, bubbling forth his melody in globules of silvery sound, and settles upon some tall tree, and waves his wings, and sinks to the swaying twigs. I hear too a quail piping from the meadow fence, and another trilling his answering whistle from the hills. Nearer by, a tyrant king-bird is poised on the topmost branch of a veteran pear-tree; and now and then dashes down assassin-like, upon some home-bound, honey-laden bee, and then, with a smack of his bill, resumes his predatory watch.

A chicken or two lie in the sun, with a wing and a leg stretched out,—lazily picking at the gravel, or relieving their ennui from time to time, with a spasmodic rustle of their feathers. An old, matronly hen stalks about the yard with a sedate step; and with quiet self-assurance, she utters an occasional series of hoarse, and heated clucks. A speckled turkey, with an astonished brood at her heels, is eyeing curiously, and with earnest variations of the head, a full-fed cat, that lies curled up, and dozing, upon the floor of the cottage porch.

As I sit thus, watching through the interstices of my leafy screen the various images of country life, I hear distant mutterings from beyond the hills.

The sun has thrown its shadow upon the pewter dial, two hours beyond the meridian line. Great cream-colored heads of thunder clouds are lifting above the sharp, clear line of the western horizon: the light breeze dies away, and the air becomes stifling, even under the shadow of my withered boughs in the chamber window. The white-capped clouds roll up nearer and nearer to the sun; and the creamy masses below grow dark in their seams. The mutterings that came faintly before, now spread into wide volumes of rolling sound, that echo again, and again, from the eastward heights.

I hear in the deep intervals, the men shouting to their teams in the meadows; and great companies of startled swallows are dashing in all directions around the gray roofs of the barn.

The clouds have now well nigh reached the sun, which seems to shine the fiercer for his coming eclipse. The whole West, as I look from the sources of the brook, to its lazy drift under the swamps that lie to the South, is hung with a curtain of darkness; and like swift-working, golden ropes that lift it toward the Zenith, long chains of lightning flash through it; and the growing thunder seems like the rumble of the pulleys.

I thrust away my azalia boughs, and fling back the shattered blinds as the sun and the clouds meet; and my room darkens with the coming shadows. For an instant, the edges of the thick creamy masses of cloud are gilded by the shrouded sun, and show gorgeous scollops of gold, that toss upon the hem of the storm. But the blazonry fades as the clouds mount; and the brightening lines of the lightning dart up from the lower skirts, and heave the billowy masses into the middle Heaven.

The workmen are urging their oxen fast across the meadow; and the loiterers come straggling after, with rakes upon their shoulders. The matronly hen has retreated to the stable door; and the brood of turkeys stand, dressing their feathers, under the open shed.

The air freshens, and blows now from the face of the coming clouds. I see the great elms in the plain swaying their tops, even before the storm breeze has reached me; and a bit of ripened grain upon a swell of the meadow, waves and tosses like a billowy sea.

Presently, I hear the rush of the wind; and the cherry and pear trees rustle through all their leaves; and my paper is whisked away by the intruding blast.

There is a quiet of a moment, in which the wind even seems weary and faint; and nothing finds utterance save one hoarse tree-toad, doling out his lugubrious notes.

Now comes a blinding flash from the clouds; and a quick, sharp clang clatters through the heavens, and bellows loud, and long among the hills. Then,—like great grief, spending its pent agony in tears—come the big drops of rain :—pattering on the lawn, and on the leaves, and most musically of all, upon the roof above me;—not now, with the light fall of the SPRING shower, but with strong steppings—like the first proud tread of YOUTH!

I.
Cloister Life.

IT has very likely occurred to you, my reader, that I am playing the wanton in these sketches; —and am breaking through all the canons of the writers, in making You my hero.

It is even so; for my work is a story of those vague feelings, doubts, passions, which belong more or less to every man of us all; and therefore it is, that I lay upon your shoulders the burden of these dreams. If this or that one never belonged to your experience,—have patience for a while. I feel sure that others are coming, which will lie like the truth upon your heart; and draw you unwittingly—perhaps tearfully even—into the belief that You are indeed my hero.

The scene now changes to the cloister of a college;—not the gray, classic cloisters which lie along the banks of the Cam or the Isis—huge, battered hulks, on whose weather-stained decks, great captains of learning have fought away their lives; nor yet the cavernous, quadrangular courts, that sleep under the dingy walls of the Sorbonne.

The youth-dreams of Clarence begin under the roof of one of those long, ungainly piles of brick and mortar, which make the colleges of New England.

The floor of the room is rough, and divided by wide seams. The study table does not stand firmly, without a few spare pennies to prop it into solid footing. The book-case of stained fir-wood, suspended against the wall by cords, is meagrely stocked, with a couple of Lexicons, a pair of grammars, a Euclid, a Xenophon, a Homer, and a Livy. Beside these, are scattered about here and there,—a thumb-worn copy of British ballads, an odd volume of the Sketch Book, a clumsy Shakspeare, and a pocket edition of the Bible.

With such appliances, added to the half score of Professors and Tutors who preside over the awful precincts, you are to work your way up to that proud entry upon our American life, which begins with the Baccalaureate degree. There is a tingling sensation in walking first under the shadow of those walls, uncouth as they are, and in feeling that you belong to them;—that you are a member, as it were, of the body corporate, subject to an actual code of printed laws, and to actual moneyed fines—varying from a shilling, to fifty cents!

There is something exhilarating in the very consciousness of your subject state; and in the necessity of measuring your hours by the habit of such a learned community. You think back upon your respect for the lank figure of some old teacher of boy days, as a childish weakness: even the little coteries of the home fire-side lose their importance, when compared with the extraordinary sweep, and dignity of your present position.

It is pleasant to measure yourself with men; and there are those about you, who seem to your untaught eye, to be men already. Your chum, a hard-faced fellow of ten more years than you,— digging sturdily at his tasks, seems by that very community of work, to dignify your labor. You watch his cold, gray eye bending down over some theorem of Euclid, with a kind of proud companionship, in what so tasks his manliness.

It is nothing for him to quit sleep at the first tinkling of the alarm clock that hangs in your chamber; or to brave the weather, in that cheerless run to the morning prayers of winter. Yet, with what a dreamy horror, you wake on mornings of snow, to that tinkling alarum!—and glide in the cold and darkness, under the shadow of the college walls:—shuddering under the sharp gusts that come sweeping between the buildings;—and afterward, gathering yourself up in your cloak, to watch in a sleepy, listless maze, the flickering lamps that hang around the dreary chapel! You follow half unconsciously some tutor's rhetorical reading of a chapter of Isaiah; and then, as he closes the Bible with a flourish, your eye, half-open, catches the feeble figure of the old Domine, as he steps to the desk, and with his frail hands stretched out upon the cover of the big book, and his head leaning slightly to one side, runs through in gentle and tremulous tones, his wonted form of Invocation.

Your Division room is steaming with foul heat, and there is a strong smell of burnt feathers, and oil. A jaunty tutor with pug nose, and consequential air, steps into the room—while you all rise to show him deference,—and takes his place at the pulpit-like desk. Then come the formal loosing of his camlet cloak clasp,—the opening of his sweaty Xenophon, to where the day's *parasangs* begin,—the unsliding of his silver pencil case,—the keen, sour look around the benches, and the cool pinch of his thumb and forefinger, into the fearful box of names!

How you listen for each as it is uttered,—running down the page in advance,—rejoicing when some hard passage comes to a stout man in the corner; and what a sigh of relief—on mornings after you have been out late at night,—when the last paragraph is reached,—the ballot drawn, and—you, safe!

You speculate dreamily upon the faces around you. You wonder what sort of schooling they may have had, and what sort of homes. You think one man has got an extraordinary name; and another, a still more extraordinary nose. The glib, easy way of one student, and his perfect *sang-froid*, completely charm you: you set him down in your own mind as a kind of Crichton. Another weazen-faced, pinched-up fellow in a scant cloak, you think must have been sometime a school-master: he is so very precise, and wears such an indescribable look of the ferule. There is one big student, with a huge beard, and a rollicking good-natured eye, whom you would quite like to see measure strength with your old usher; and on careful comparison, rather think the usher would get the worst of it. Another appears as venerable as some fathers you have seen; and it seems wonderfully odd, that a man old enough to have children, should recite Xenophon by morning candle-light!

The class in advance, you study curiously; and are quite amazed at the precocity of certain youths belonging to it, who are apparently about your own age. The Juniors you look upon, with a quiet reverence for their aplomb, and dignity of character; and look forward with intense yearnings, to the time when you, too, shall be admitted freely to the precincts of the Philosophical chamber, and to the very steep benches of the Laboratory. This last seems, from occasional peeps through the blinds, a most mysterious building. The chimneys, recesses, vats, and cisterns—to say nothing of certain galvanic communications, which you are told, traverse the whole building—in a way capable of killing a rat, at an incredible remove from the bland professor,—utterly fatigue your wonder! You humbly trust—though you have doubts upon the point—that you will have the capacity to grasp it all, when once you shall have arrived at the dignity of a Junior.

As for the Seniors, your admiration for them is entirely boundless. In one or two individual instances, it is true, it has been broken down, by an unfortunate squabble, with thick set fellows in the Chapel aisle. A person who sits not far before you at prayers, and whose name you seek out very early, bears a strong resemblance to some portrait of Dr. Johnson; you have very much the same kind of respect for him, that you feel for the great lexicographer; and do not for a moment doubt his capacity to compile a Dictionary equal if not superior to Johnson's.

Another man with very bushy, black hair, and an easy look of importance, carries a large cane; and is represented to you, as an astonishing scholar, and speaker. You do not doubt it; his very air proclaims it. You think of him, as, presently— (say four or five years hence)—astounding the United States Senate with his eloquence. And when once you have heard him in debate, with that ineffable gesture of his, you absolutely languish in your admiration for him; and you describe his speaking to your country friends, as very little inferior, if any, to Mr. Burke's. Beside this one, are some half dozen others, among whom the question of superiority is, you understand, strongly mooted. It puzzles you to think, what an avalanche of talent will fall upon the country, at the graduation of those Seniors!

You will find, however, that the country bears such inundations of college talent, with a remarkable degree of equanimity. It is quite wonderful how all the Burkes, and Scotts, and Peels, among college Seniors, do quietly disappear, as a man gets on in life.

As for any degree of fellowship with such giants, t is an honor hardly to be thought of. But you have a classmate—I will call him Dalton,—who is very intimate with a dashing Senior; they room near each other outside the college. You quite envy Dalton, and you come to know him well. He says that you are not a 'green-one,'—that you have 'cut your eye teeth;' in return for which complimentary opinions, you entertain a strong friendship for Dalton.

He is a 'fast' fellow, as the Senior calls him; and it is a proud thing to happen at their rooms occasionally, and to match yourself for an hour or two (with the windows darkened) against a Senior at 'old sledge.' It is quite 'the thing,' as Dalton says, to meet a Senior familiarly in the street. Sometimes you go, after Dalton has taught you 'the ropes,' to have a cosy sit-down over oysters and champagne;—to which the Senior lends himself, with the pleasantest condescension in the world. You are not altogether used to hard drinking; but this, you conceal,—as most spirited young fellows do,—by drinking a great deal. You have a dim recollection of certain circumstances— very unimportant, yet very vividly impressed on your mind,—which occurred on one of these occa sions.

The oysters were exceedingly fine, and the champagne—exquisite. You have a recollection of something being said, toward the end of the first bottle, of Xenophon, and of the Senior's saying in his playful way,—' Oh, d—n Xenophon!'

You remember Dalton laughed at this; and you laughed—for company. You remember that you thought, and Dalton thought, and the Senior thought—by a singular coincidence, that the second bottle of champagne was better even than the first. You have a dim remembrance of the Senior's saying very loudly, " Clarence—(calling you by your family name) is no spooney;" and drinking a bumper with you in confirmation of the remark.

You remember that Dalton broke out into a song, and that for a time you joined in the chorus; you think the Senior called you to order for repeating the chorus, in the wrong place. You think the lights burned with remarkable brilliancy; and you remember that a remark of yours to that effect, met with very much such a response from the Senior, as he had before employed with reference to Xenophon.

You have a confused idea of calling Dalton—Xenophon. You think the meeting broke up with a chorus; and that somebody—you cannot tell who—broke two or three glasses. You remember questioning yourself very seriously, as to whether you were or were not, tipsy. You think you decided that you were not, but—might be.

You have a confused recollection of leaning

upon some one, or something, going to your room, this sense of a desire to lean, you think, was very strong. You remember being horribly afflicted with the idea of having tried your night key at the tutor's door, instead of your own; you remember further a hot stove,—made certain indeed, by a large blister which appeared on your hand, next day. You think of throwing off your clothes, by one or two spasmodic efforts,—leaning in the intervals, against the bed-post.

There is a recollection of an uncommon dizziness afterward—as if your body was very quiet, and your head gyrating with strange velocity, and a kind of centrifugal action, all about the room, and the college, and indeed the whole town. You think that you felt uncontrollable nausea after this, followed by positive sickness;—which waked your chum, who thought you very incoherent, and feared derangement.

A dismal state of lassitude follows, broken by the college clock striking three, and by very rambling reflections upon champagne, Xenophon, 'Captain Dick,' Madge, and the old deacon who clinched his wig in the church.

The next morning—(ah, how vexatious that all our follies are followed by a—' next morning!') you wake with a parched mouth, and a torturing thirst; the sun is shining broadly into your reeking chamber. Prayers and recitations are long ago over; and you see through the door, in the outer room, that hard faced chum, with his Lexicon, and

Livy, open before him, working out with all the earnestness of his iron purpose, the steady steps toward preferment, and success.

You go with some story of sudden sickness to the Tutor;—half fearful that the bloodshot, swollen eyes will betray you. It is very mortifying too, to meet Dalton appearing so gay, and lively after it all, while you wear such an air of being 'used up.' You envy him thoroughly the extraordinary capacity that he has.

Here and there creeps in, amid all the pride and shame of the new life, a tender thought of the old home; but its joys are joys no longer: its highest aspirations even, have resolved themselves into fine mist,—like rainbows, that the sun drinks with his beams.

The affection for a mother, whose kindness you recall with a suffused eye, is not gone, or blighted; but it is woven up, as only a single adorning tissue, into the growing pride of youth: it is cherished in the proud soul, rather as a redeeming weakness, than as a vital energy.

And the love for Nelly, though it bates no jot of fervor, is woven into the scale of growing purposes, rather as a color to adorn, than as a strand to strengthen.

As for your other loves, those romantic ones, which were kindled by bright eyes, and the stolen reading of Miss Porter's novels, they linger on your mind like perfumes; and they float down your memory, with the figure, the step, the last words of those young girls, who raised them,—like the types of some dimly-shadowed, but deeper passion, which is some time to spur your maturer purposes, and to quicken your manly resolves.

It would be hard to tell, for you do not as yet know, but that Madge herself,—hoydenish, blue-eyed Madge, is to be the very one who will gain such hold upon your riper affections, as she has held already over your boyish caprice. It is a part of the pride,—I may say rather an evidence of the pride, which youth feels in leaving boyhood behind him, to talk laughingly, and carelessly, of those attachments which made his young years so balmy with dreams.

II.

First Ambition.

I BELIEVE that sooner or later, there come to every man, dreams of ambition. They may be covered with the sloth of habit, or with a pretence of humility: they may come only in dim, shadowy visions, that feed the eye like the glories of an ocean sun-rise; but, you may be sure that they will come: even before one is aware, the bold, adventurous Goddess, whose name is Ambition, and whose dower is Fame, will be toying with the feeble heart. And she pushes her ventures with a bold hand: she makes timidity strong, and weakness valiant.

The way of a man's heart will be foreshadowed by what goodness lies in him,—coming from above, and from around;—but a way foreshadowed, is not a way made. And the making of a man's way, comes only from that quickening of resolve, which we call Ambition. It is the spur that makes man struggle with Destiny; it is Heaven's own incentive, to make Purpose great, and Achievement greater.

It would be strange if you, in that cloister life of a college, did not sometimes feel a dawning of new resolves. They grapple you indeed, oftener than you dare to speak of. Here, you dream first of that very sweet, but very shadowy success, called reputation.

You think of the delight and astonishment, it would give your mother and father, and most of all, little Nelly, if you were winning such honors, as now escape you. You measure your capacities by those about you, and watch their habit of study; you gaze for a half hour together, upon some successful man, who has won his prizes; and wonder by what secret action he has done it. And when, in time, you come to be a competitor yourself, your anxiety is immense.

You spend hours upon hours at your theme. You write and re-write; and when it is at length complete, and out of your hands, you are harassed by a thousand doubts. At times, as you recall your hours of toil, you question if so much has been spent upon any other; you feel almost certain of success. You repeat to yourself, some passages of special eloquence, at night. You fancy the admiration of the Professors at meeting with such wonderful performance. You have a slight fear that its superior goodness may awaken the suspicion, that some one out of the college—some superior man, may have written it. But this fear dies away.

The eventful day is a great one in your calendar; you hardly sleep the night previous. You tremble as the Chapel bell is rung; you profess to be very indifferent, as the reading and the prayer close; you even stoop to take up your hat,—as if you had entirely overlooked the fact, that the old President was in the desk, for the express purpose of declaring the successful names. You listen dreamily to his tremulous, yet fearfully distinct enunciation. Your head swims strangely.

They all pass out with a harsh murmur, along the aisles, and through the door ways. It would be well if there were no disappointments in life more terrible than this. It is consoling to express very deprecating opinions of the Faculty in general;—and very contemptuous ones of that particular officer who decided upon the merit of the prize themes. An evening or two at Dalton's room go still farther toward healing the disappointment; and—if it must be said—toward moderating the heat of your ambition.

You grow up however, unfortunately, as the College years fly by, into a very exaggerated sense of your own capacities. Even the good, old, white-haired Squire, for whom you had once entertained so much respect, seems to your crazy, classic fancy, a very hum-drum sort of personage. Frank, although as noble a fellow as ever sat a horse, is yet—you cannot help thinking—very ignorant of Euripides; even the English master at Dr. Bidlow's school, you feel sure, would balk at a dozen problems you could give him.

You get an exalted idea of that uncertain quality, which turns the heads of a vast many of your fellows, called—Genius. An odd notion seems to be inherent in the atmosphere of those College chambers, that there is a certain faculty of mind— first developed as would seem in Colleges,—which accomplishes whatever it chooses, without any special pains-taking. For a time, you fall yourself into this very unfortunate hallucination; you cultivate it, after the usual college fashion, by drinking a vast deal of strong coffee, and whiskey toddy,— by writing a little poor verse, in the Byronic temper, and by studying very late at night, with closed blinds.

It costs you, however, more anxiety and hypocrisy than you could possibly have believed.

——You will learn, Clarence, when the Autumn has rounded your hopeful Summer, if not before, that there is no Genius in life, like the Genius of energy and industry. You will learn, that all the traditions so current among very young men, that certain great characters have wrought their greatness by an inspiration as it were, grow out of a sad mistake.

And you will further find, when you come to measure yourself with men, that there are no rivals so formidable, as those earnest, determined minds, which reckon the value of every hour, and which achieve eminence by persistent application.

Literary ambition may inflame you at certain periods; and a thought of some great names will flash like a spark into the mine of your purposes; you dream till midnight over books; you set up shadows, and chase them down—other shadows, and they fly. Dreaming will never catch them. Nothing makes the 'scent lie well,' in the hunt after distinction, but labor.

And it is a glorious thing, when once you are weary of the dissipation, and the ennui of your own aimless thought, to take up some glowing page of an earnest thinker, and read—deep and long, until you feel the metal of his thought tinkling on your brain, and striking out from your flinty lethargy, flashes of ideas, that give the mind light and heat. And away you go, in the chase of what the soul within is creating on the instant, and you wonder at the fecundity of what seemed so barren, and at the ripeness of what seemed so crude. The glow of toil wakes you to the consciousness of your real capacities: you feel sure that they have taken a new step toward final development. In such mood it is, that one feels grateful to the musty tomes, which at other hours stand like curiosity-making mummies, with no warmth, and no vitality. Now they grow into the affections like new-found friends; and gain a hold upon the heart, and light a fire in the brain, that the years and the mould cannot cover, nor quench.

III.

College Romance.

IN following the mental vagaries of youth, I must not forget the curvetings and wiltings of the heart.

The black-eyed Jenny, with whom a correspondence at red heat was kept up for several weeks, is long before this, entirely out of your regard;—not so much by reason of the six months' disparity of age, as from the fact, communicated quite confidentially by the travelled Nat, that she has had a desperate flirtation with a handsome midshipman. The conclusion is natural, that she is an inconstant, cruel-hearted creature, with little appreciation of real worth; and furthermore, that all midshipmen are a very contemptible, not to say,—dangerous set of men. She is consigned to forgetfulness and neglect; and the late lover has long ago consoled himself, by reading in a spirited way, that passage of Childe Harold, commencing,—

I have not loved the world, nor the world me.

As for Madge, the memory of her has been more wakeful, but less violent. To say nothing of occasional returns to the old homestead when you have met her, Nelly's letters not unfrequently drop a careless half-sentence, that keeps her strangely in mind.

'Madge,' she says, 'is sitting by me with her work;' or, 'you ought to see the little, silk purse that Madge is knitting;' or, speaking of some country rout—'Madge was there in the sweetest dress you can imagine.' All this will keep Madge in mind; not it is true in the ambitious moods, or in the frolic with Dalton; but in those odd half hours that come stealing over one at twilight, laden with sweet memories of the days of old.

A new Romantic admiration is started by those pale lady-faces which light up, on a Sunday, the gallery of the college chapel. An amiable and modest fancy, gives to them all a sweet classic grace. The very atmosphere of those courts, wakened with high metaphysic discourse, seems to lend them a Greek beauty, and finesse; and you attach to the prettiest that your eye can reach, all the charms of some Sciote maiden, and all the learning of her father—the Professor. And as you lie half-wakeful, and half-dreaming, through the long Divisions of the Doctor's morning discourse, the twinkling eyes in some corner of the gallery, bear you pleasant company, as you float down those streaming visions, which radiate from you far over the track of the coming life.

But following very closely upon this, comes a whole volume of street romance. There are prettily shaped figures that go floating, at convenient hours for college observation, along the thoroughfares of the town. And these figures come to be known, and the dresses, and the streets; and even the door-plate is studied. The hours are ascertained, by careful observation and induction, at which some particular figure is to be met; or is to be seen at some low parlor window, in white summer dress, with head leaning on the hand,—very melancholy, and very dangerous. Perhaps her very card is stuck proudly into a corner of the mirror, in the college chamber. After this may come moonlight meetings at the gate, or long listenings to the plaintive lyrics that steal out of the parlor windows, and that blur wofully the text of the Conic Sections.

Or, perhaps she is under the fierce eye of some Cerberus of a school-mistress, about whose grounds you prowl piteously, searching for small knot holes in the surrounding board-fence, through which little souvenirs of impassioned feeling may be thrust. Sonnets are written for the town papers, full of telling phrases, and with classic allusions, and foot notes, which draw attention to some similar felicity of expression in Horace, or Ovid. Correspondence may even be ventured on, enclosing locks of hair, and interchanging rings, and paper oaths of eternal fidelity.

But the old Cerberus is very wakeful: **the let**

ters fail: the lamp that used to glimmer for a sign among the sycamores, is gone out: a stolen wave of a handkerchief,—a despairing look,—and tears, which you fancy, but do not see,—make you miserable for long days.

The tyrant teacher, with no trace of compassion in her withered heart, reports you to the college authorities. There is a long lecture of admonition upon the folly of such dangerous practices; and if the offence be aggravated by some recent joviality with Dalton and the Senior, you are condemned to a month of exile with a country clergyman. There are a few tearful regrets over the painful tone of the home letters; but the bracing country air, and the pretty faces of the village girls heal your heart, —with fresh wounds.

The old Doctor sees dimly through his spectacles; and his pew gives a good look out upon the smiling choir of singers. A collegian wears the honors of a stranger; and the country bucks stand but poor chance in contrast with your wonderful attainments in cravats and verses. But this fresh dream, odorous with its memories of sleigh-rides, or lilac blossoms, slips by, and yields again to the more ambitious dreams of the cloister.

In the prouder moments that come, when you are more a man, and less a boy—with more of strategy and less of faith—your thought of woman runs loftily: not loftily in the realm of virtue or goodness, but loftily on your new world-scale. The pride of intellect that is thirsting in you, fashions

Ideal graces after a classic model. The heroines of fable are admired; and the soul is tortured with that intensity of passion, which gleams through the broken utterances of Grecian tragedy.

In the vanity of self-consciousness, one feels at a long remove above the ordinary love and trustfulness of a simple and pure heart. You turn away from all such with a sigh of conceit, to graze on that lofty, but bitter pasturage, where no daisies grow. Admiration may be called up by some graceful figure that you see moving under those sweeping elms; and you follow it with an intensity of look that makes you blush; and straightway, hide the memory of the blush, by summing up some artful sophistry, that resolves your delighted gaze into a weakness, and your contempt into a virtue.

But this cannot last. As the years drop off, a certain pair of eyes beam one day upon you, that seem to have been cut out of a page of Greek poetry. They have all its sentiment, its fire, its intellectual reaches: it would be hard to say what they have not. The profile is a Greek profile; and the heavy chestnut hair is plaited in Greek bands. The figure too, might easily be that of Helen, or of Andromache.

You gaze—ashamed to gaze; and your heart yearns—ashamed of its yearning. It is no young girl, who is thus testing you: there is too much pride for that. A ripeness and maturity rest upon her look, and figure, that completely fill up that ideal, which exaggerated fancies have wrought out of the Grecian heaven. The vision steals upon you at all hours,—now rounding its flowing outline to the mellifluous metre of Epic Hexameter, and again, with its bounding life, pulsating with the glorious dashes of tragic verse.

Yet, with the exception of stolen glances, and secret admiration, you keep aloof. There is no wish to fathom what seems a happy mystery There lies a content in secret obeisance. Sometimes it shames you as your mind glows with its fancied dignity; but the heart thrusts in its voice; and yielding to it, you dream dreams, like fond, old Boccacio's, upon the olive-shaded slopes of Italy. The tongue even is not trusted with the thoughts that are seething within: they begin and end in the voiceless pulsations of your nature.

After a time,—it seems a long time, but it is in truth, a very short time,—you find who she is, who is thus entrancing you. It is done most carelessly. No creature could imagine that you felt any interest in the accomplished sister—of your friend Dalton. Yet it is even she, who has thus beguiled you; and she is at least some ten years Dalton's senior; and by even more years,—your own!

It is singular enough, but it is true,—that the affections of that transition state from youth to manliness, run toward the types of maturity. The mind in its reaches toward strength, and completeness, creates a heart-sympathy—which, in its turn, craves fullness. There is a vanity too about the first steps of manly education, which is disposed to under-rate the innocence, and unripened judgment of the other sex. Men see the mistake, as they grow older;—for the judgment of a woman, in all matters of the affections, ripens by ten years, faster than a man's.

In place of any relentings on such score, you are set on fire anew. The stories of her accomplishments, and of her grace of conversation, absolutely drive you mad. You watch your occasion for meeting her upon the street. You wonder if she has any conception of your capacity for mental labor; and if she has any adequate idea of your admiration for Greek poetry, and for herself?

You tie your cravat poet-wise, and wear broad collars, turned down, wondering how such disposition may affect her. Her figure and step become a kind of moving romance to you, drifting forward, and outward into that great land of dreams, which you call the world. When you see her walking with others, you pity her; and feel perfectly sure that if she had only a hint of that intellectual fervor which, in your own mind, blazes up at the very thought of her, she would perfectly scorn the stout gentleman who spends his force in tawdry compliments.

A visit to your home awakens ardor, by contrast, as much as by absence. Madge, so gentle, and now stealing sly looks at you, in a way so different from her hoydenish manner of school-days, you regard complacently, as a most lovable, fond girl—the very one for some fond and amiable young man, whose soul is not filled—as yours is—with higher things! To Nelly, earnestly listening, you drop only exaggerated hints of the wonderful beauty, and dignity of this new being of your fancy. Of her age, you scrupulously say nothing.

The trivialities of Dalton amaze you; it is hard to understand how a man within the limit of such influence, as Miss Dalton must inevitably exert, can tamely sit down to a rubber of whist, and cigars! There must be a sad lack of congeniality; it would certainly be a proud thing to supply that lack!

The new feeling, wild and vague as it is,—for as yet, you have only most casual acquaintance with Laura Dalton,—invests the whole habit of your study; not quickening overmuch the relish for Dugald Stewart, or the miserable skeleton of college Logic; but spending a sweet charm upon the graces of Rhetoric, and the music of Classic Verse. It blends harmoniously with your quickened ambition. There is some last appearance that you have to make upon the College stage, in the presence of the great worthies of the State, and of all the beauties of the town,—Laura chiefest among them. In view of it, you feel dismally intellectual. Prodigious faculties are to be brought to the task.

You think of throwing out ideas that will quite startle His Excellency the Governor, and those very distinguished public characters, whom the College purveyors vote into their periodic public sittings. You are quite sure of surprising them, and of deeply provoking such scheming, shallow politicians, as have never read 'Wayland's Treatise;' and who venture incautiously within hearing of your remarks. You fancy yourself in advance, the victim of a long leader in the next day's paper; and the thoughtful, but quiet cause of a great change in the political programme of the State. But crowning and eclipsing all the triumph, are those dark eyes beaming on you from some corner of the Church, their floods of unconscious praise and tenderness.

Your father and Nelly are there to greet you. He has spoken a few calm, quiet words of encouragement that make you feel—very wrongfully—that he is a cold man, with no earnestness of feeling. As for Nelly, she clasps your arm with a fondness, and with a pride, that tell at every step, her praises and her love.

But even this, true and healthful as it is, fades before a single word of commendation from the new arbitress of your feeling. You have seen Miss Dalton! You have met her on that last evening of your cloistered life, in all the elegance of ball costume; your eye has feasted on her elegant figure, and upon her eye sparkling with the consciousness of beauty. You have talked with Miss Dalton about Byron,—about Wordsworth,—about Homer. You have quoted poetry to Miss Dalton; you have clasped Miss Dalton's hand!

Her conversation delights you by its piquancy

and grace ; she is quite ready to meet you (a grave matter of surprise !) upon whatever subject you may suggest. You lapse easily and lovingly into the current of her thought, and blush to find yourself vacantly admiring, when she is looking for reply. The regard you feel for her, resolves itself into an exquisite mental love, vastly superior as you think, to any other kind of love. There is no dream of marriage as yet, but only of sitting beside her in the moonlight, during a countless succession of hours, and talking of poetry and nature,—of destiny, and love.

Magnificent Miss Dalton.

——And all the while, vaunting youth is almost mindless of the presence of that fond Nelly, whose warm sisterly affection measures itself hopefully against the proud associations of your growing years ; and whose deep, loving eye half suffused with its native tenderness, seems longing to win you back to the old joys of that Home-love, which linger on the distant horizon of your boy-hood, like the golden glories of a sinking day.

As the night wanes, you wander, for a last look, toward the dingy walls, that have made for you so long a home. The old broken expectancies, the days of glee, the triumphs, the rivalries, the defeats, the friendships, are recalled with a fluttering of the heart, that pride cannot wholly subdue. You step upon the Chapel-porch, in the quiet of the night, as you would step on the graves of friends. You pace back and forth in the wan moonlight, dreaming of that dim life which opens wide and long, from the morrow. The width and length oppress you: they crush down your struggling self-consciousness, like Titans dealing with Pigmies. A single piercing thought of the vast and shadowy future which is so near, tears off on the instant all the gew-gaws of pride,—strips away the vanity that doubles your bigness, and forces you down to the bare nakedness of what you truly *are!*

With one more yearning look at the gray hulks of building, you loiter away under the trees. The monster elms which have bowered your proud steps through four years of proudest life, lift up to the night their rounded canopy of leaves, with a quiet majesty that mocks you. They kiss the same calm sky, which they wooed four years ago; and they droop their trailing limbs lovingly to the same earth, which has steadily, and quietly, wrought in them their stature, and their strength. Only here and there, you catch the loitering foot-fall of some other benighted dreamer, strolling around the vast quadrangle of level green, which lies like a prairie-child, under the edging shadows of the town. The lights glimmer one by one; and one by one—like breaking hopes—they fade away from the houses. The full risen moon that dapples the ground beneath the trees, touches the tall church spires with silver; and slants their loftiness—as memory slants grief—in long, dark, tapering lines, upon the silvered Green.

IV.

First Look at the World.

OUR Clarence is now fairly afloat upon the swift tide of Youth. The thrall of teachers is ended, and the audacity of self-resolve is begun. It is not a little odd, that when we have least strength to combat the world, we have the highest confidence in our ability.

Very few individuals in the world, possess that happy consciousness of their own prowess, which belongs to the newly graduated Collegian. He has most abounding faith in the tricksy panoply that he has wrought out of the metal of his Classics. His mathematics, he has not a doubt, will solve for him every complexity of life's questions; and his logic will as certainly untie all gordian knots, whether in politics or ethics.

He has no idea of defeat; he proposes to take the world by storm; he half wonders that quiet people are not startled by his presence. He brushes with an air of importance about the halls of country hotels; he wears his honor at the public tables; he fancies that the inattentive guests can have little idea that the young gentleman, who so recently delighted the public ear with his dissertation on the " General tendency of Opinion," is actually among them; and quietly eating from the same dish of beef, and of pudding!

Our poor Clarence does not know—heaven forbid he should!—that he is but little wiser now, than when he turned his back upon the old Academy, with its gallipots, and broken retorts; and that with the addition of a few Greek roots, a smattering of Latin, and some readiness of speech, he is almost as weak for breasting the strong current of life, as when a boy. America is but a poor place for the romantic book-dreamer. The demands of this new, Western life of ours, are practical, and earnest. Prompt action, and ready tact, are the weapons by which to meet it, and subdue it. The education of the cloister offers at best, only a sound starting point, from which to leap into the tide.

The father of Clarence is a cool, matter-of-fact man. He has little sympathy with any of the romantic notions that enthrall a youth of twenty. He has a very humble opinion—much humbler than you think he ought—of your attainments at College. He advises a short period of travel, that by observation, you may find out more, how that world is made up, with which you are henceforth to struggle.

Your mother half fears your alienation from the

affections of home. Her letters all run over with a tenderness that makes you sigh, and that makes you feel a deep reproach. You may not have been wanting in the more ordinary tokens of affection; you have made your periodic visits; but you blush for the consciousness that fastens on you, of neglect at heart. You blush for the lack of that glow of feeling, which once fastened to every home-object.

[Does a man indeed outgrow affections as his mind ripens? Do the early and tender sympathies become a part of his intellectual perceptions, to be appreciated and reasoned upon, as one reasons about truths of science? Is their vitality necessarily young? Is there the same ripe, joyous burst of the heart at the recollection of later friendships, which belonged to those of boyhood; and are not the later ones more the suggestions of judgment, and less, the absolute conditions of the heart's health?]

The letters of your mother, as I said, make you sigh: there is no moment in our lives when we feel less worthy of the love of others, and less worthy of our own respect, than when we receive evidences of kindness, which we know we do not merit; and when souls are laid bare to us, and we have too much indifference to lay bare our own in return.

"Clarence"—writes that neglected mother—" you do not know how much you are in our thoughts, and how often you are the burden of my prayers. Oh, Clarence, I could almost wish that you were still a boy—still running to me for those little favors, which I was only too happy to bestow, —still dependent in some degree on your mother's love, for happiness.

"Perhaps I do you wrong, Clarence, but it does seem from the changing tone of your letters that you are becoming more and more forgetful of us all;— that you are feeling less need of our advice, and— what I feel far more deeply—less need of our affection. Do not, my son, forget the lessons of home. There will come a time, I feel sure, when you will know that those lessons are good. They may not indeed help you in that intellectual strife which soon will engross you; and they may not have fitted you to shine in what are called the brilliant circles of the world; but they are such, Clarence, as make the heart pure, and honest, and strong!

"You may think me weak to write you thus, as I would have written to my light-hearted boy, years ago;—indeed I am not strong, but growing every day more feeble.

"Nelly, your sweet sister, is sitting by me: 'Tell Clarence,' she says, 'to come home soon.' You know, my son, what hearty welcome will greet you; and that whether here, or away, our love and prayers will be with you always; and may God, in his infinite mercy, keep you from all harm!"

A tear or two,—brushed away, as soon as they come,—is all that youth gives, to embalm such treasure of love! A gay laugh, or the challenge of some companion of a day, will sweep away into the night, the earnest, regretful, yet happy dreams, that rise like incense from the pages of such hallowed affection.

The brusque world too is to be met, with all its hurry and promptitude. Manhood, in our swift American world, is measured too much by forgetfulness of all the sweet liens which tie the heart to the home of its first attachments. We deaden the glow that nature has kindled, lest it may lighten our hearts into an enchanting flame of weakness. We have not learned to make that flame the beacon of our purposes, and the warmer of our strength. We are men too early.

But an experience is approaching Clarence, that will drive his heart home for shelter, like a wounded bird!

——It is an autumn morning, with such crimson glories to kindle it, as lie along the twin ranges of mountain that guard the Hudson. The white frosts shine like changing silk, in the fields of late growing clover; the river mists curl, and idle along the bosom of the water, and creep up the hill sides; and at noon, float their feathery vapors aloft, in clouds; the crimson trees blaze in the side valleys, and blend their vermillion tints under the fairy hands of our American frost-painters, with the dark blood of the ash trees, and the orange tinted oaks. Blue and bright, under the clear Fall heaven, the broad river shines before the surging prow of the boat, like a shield of steel.

The bracing air lights up rich dreams of life. Your fancy peoples the valleys, and the hill-tops with its creations; and your hope lends some crowning beauty of the landscape, to your dreamy future. The vision of your last college year is not gone. That figure whose elegance your eyes then feasted on, still floats before you; and the memory of the last talk with Laura, is as vivid, as if it were only yesterday, that you listened. Indeed, this opening campaign of travel,—although you are half ashamed to confess it to yourself,—is guided by the thought of her.

Dalton, with a party of friends, his sister among them, are journeying to the north. A hope of meeting them—scarce acknowledged as an intention—spurs you on. The eye rests dreamily, and vaguely on the beauties that appear at every turn: they are beauties that charm you, and charm you the more by an indefinable association with that fairy object that floats before you, half unknown, and wholly unclaimed. The quiet towns, with their noon-day stillness, the out-lying mansions with their stately splendor, the bustling cities with their mocking din, and the long reaches of silent, and wooded shore, chime with their several beauties to your heart, in keeping with the master key, that was touched long weeks before.

The cool, honest advices of the father, drift across your memory in shadowy forms, as you wander through the streets of the first northern cities; and all the need for observation, and the incentives to purpose, which your ambitious designs would once have quickened, fade dismally, when you find that *she* is not there. All the lax gaiety of Saratoga palls on the appetite: even the magnificent shores of Lake George, though stirring your spirit to an insensible wonder and love, do not cheat you into a trance that lingers. In vain, the sun blazons every isle, and lights every shaded cove, and at evening, stretches the Black mountain in giant slumber on the waters.

Your thought bounds away from the beauty of sky and lake, and fastens upon the ideal which your dreamy humors cherish. The very glow of pursuit heightens your fervor:—a fervor that dims sadly the new-wakened memories of home. The southern gates of Champlain, those fir-draped Trosachs of America, are passed, and you find yourself upon a golden evening of Canadian autumn, in the quaint old city of Montreal.

Dalton, with his party, has gone down to Quebec. He is to return within a few days, on his way to Niagara. There is a letter from Nelly waiting you. It says:—'Mother is much more feeble: she often speaks of your return, in a way that I am sure, if you heard, Clarence, would bring you back to us soon.'

There is a struggle in your mind: old affection is weaker than young pride and hope. Moreover, the world is to be faced: the new scenes around you are to be studied. An answer is penned full of kind remembrances, and begging a few days of delay. You wander, wondering, under the quaint old houses, and wishing for the return of Dalton.

He meets you with that happy, careless way of his—the dangerous way which some men are born to,—and which chimes easily to every tone of the world :—a way you wondered at once; a way, you admire now, and a way that you will distrust, as you come to see more of men. Miss Dalton—(it seems sacrilege to call her Laura)—is the same elegant being that entranced you first.

They urge you to join their party. But there is no need of urgence: those eyes, that figure, the whole presence indeed of Miss Dalton, attract you with a power which you can neither explain, nor resist. One look of grace enslaves you; and there is a strange pride in the enslavement.

——Is it dream, or is it earnest,—those moon-lit walks upon the hills that skirt the city, when you watch the stars, listening to her voice, and feel the pressure of that jewelled hand upon your arm ?—when you drain your memory of its whole stock of poetic beauties, to lavish upon her ear ? Is it love, or is it madness, when you catch her eye, as it beams more of eloquence than lies in all your moonlight poetry, and feel an exultant gush of the heart, that makes you proud as a man, and yet timid as a boy, beside her ?

Has Dalton with that calm, placid, nonchalant look of his, any inkling of the raptures, which his elegant sister is exciting ? Has the stout, elderly gentleman who is so prodigal of his bouquets, and attentions, any idea of the formidable rival that he has found ? Has Laura herself—you dream—any conception of that intensity of admiration with which you worship?

——Poor Clarence! it is his first look at Life!

The Thousand Isles with their leafy beauties, lie around your passing boat, like the joys that skirt us, and pass us, on our way through life. The Thousand Isles rise sudden before you, and fringe your yeasty track, and drop away into floating spectres of beauty—of haze—of distance, like those dreams of joy, that your passion lends the brain. The low banks of Ontario look sullen by night; and the moon, rising tranquilly over the tops of vast forests that stand in majestic ranks over ten thousand acres of shore-land, drips its silvery sparkles along the rocking waters, and flashes across your foamy wake.

With such attendance, that subdues for the time the dreamy forays of your passion, you draw toward the sound of Niagara; and its distant, vague roar coming through great aisles of gloomy forest, bears up your spirit, like a child's, into the Highest Presence.

The morning after, you are standing with your party upon the steps of the Hotel. A letter is handed to you. Dalton remarks in a quizzical way, that 'it shows a lady's hand.'

"Aha, a lady!" says Miss Dalton;—and so gaily!

"A sister," I say; for it is Nelly's hand.

"By the by, Clarence," says Dalton, "it was a very pretty sister, you gave us a glimse of at commencement."

"Ah, you think so," and there is something in your tone, that shows a little indignation at this careless mention of your fond Nelly;—and from those lips! It will occur to you again.

A single glance at the letter blanches your cheek. Your heart throbs:—throbs harder,—throbs tumultuously. You bite your lip; for there are lookers on. But it will not do. You hurry away: you find your chamber: you close and lock the door, and burst into a flood of tears.

V.

A Broken Home.

IT is Nelly's own fair hand, yet sadly blotted;—blotted with her tears, and blotted with yours.

——" It is all over, dear, dear Clarence! oh, how I wish you were here to mourn with us! I can hardly now believe that our poor mother is indeed dead."

Dead!—It is a terrible word. You repeat it, with a fresh burst of grief. The letter is crumpled in your hand. Unfold it again, sobbing, and read on.

" For a week, she had been failing every day; but on Saturday, we thought her very much better. I told her, I felt sure she would live to see you again.

" ' I shall never see him again, Nelly,' said she, bursting into tears.' "

——Ah, Clarence, where is your youthful pride, and your strength now?—with only that frail paper to annoy you, crushed in your grasp!

"She sent for Father, and taking his hand in hers, told him she was dying. I am glad you did not see his grief. I was kneeling beside her, and she put her hand upon my head, and let it rest there for a moment, while her lips moved, as if she were praying.

"'Kiss me, Nelly,' said she, growing fainter: 'kiss me again for Clarence.'

"A little while after she died."

For a long time you remain with only that letter, and your thought for company. You pace up and down your chamber: again you seat yourself and lean your head upon the table, enfeebled by the very grief, that you cherish still. The whole day passes thus: you excuse yourself from all companionship: you have not the heart to tell the story of your troubles to Dalton,—least of all, to Miss Dalton. How is this? Is sorrow too selfish, or too holy?

Toward night-fall there is a calmer, and stronger feeling. The voice of the present world comes to your ear again. But you move away from it unobserved to that stronger voice of God, in the Cataract. Great masses of angry cloud hang over the West; but beneath them the red harvest sun shines over the long reach of Canadian shore, and bathes the whirling rapids in splendor. You stroll alone over the quaking bridge, and under the giant trees of the Island, to the edge of the British Fall. You go out to the little shattered tower, and gaze down with sensations that will last till death, upon the deep emerald of those awful masses of water.

It is not the place for a bad man to ponder: it is not the atmosphere for foul thoughts, or weak ones. A man is never better than when he has the humblest sense of himself: he is never so unlike the spirit of Evil, as when his pride is utterly vanished. You linger, looking upon the stream of fading sunlight that plays across the rapids, and down into the shadow of the depths below, lit up with their clouds of spray:—yet farther down, your sight swims upon the black eddying masses, with white ribands streaming across their glassy surface; and your dizzy eye fastens upon the frail cockle shells,—their stout oarsmen dwindled to pigmies,—that dance like atoms upon the vast chasm,—or like your own weak resolves upon the whirl of Time.

Your thought, growing broad in the view, seems to cover the whole area of life; you set up your affections and your duties; you build hopes with fairy scenery, and away they all go, tossing like the relentless waters to the deep gulf, that gapes a hideous welcome! You sigh at your weakness of heart, or of endeavor, and your sighs float out into the breeze that rises ever from the shock of the waves, and whirl, empty-handed, to Heaven. You avow high purposes, and clench them with round utterance; and your voice like a sparrow's, is caught up in the roar of the fall, and thrown at you from the cliffs, and dies away in the solemn thunders of nature. Great thoughts of life come over you—of its work and destiny—of its affections and duties, and roll down swift—like the river—into the deep whirl of doubt and danger. Other thoughts, grander and stronger, like the continuing rush of waters, come over you, and knit your purposes together with their weight, and crush you to exulting tears, and then leap, shattered and broken, from the very edge of your intent,—into mists of fear.

The moon comes out, and gleaming through the clouds, braids its light, fantastic bow upon the waters. You feel calmer as the night deepens. The darkness softens you; it hangs—like the pall that shrouds your mother's corpse,—low and heavily to your heart. It helps your inward grief, with some outward show. It makes the earth a mourner; it makes the flashing water-drops so many attendant mourners. It makes the Great Fall itself a mourner, and its roar—a requiem.

The pleasure of travel is cut short. To one person of the little company of fellow voyagers, you bid adieu with regret; pride, love, and hope point toward her, while all the gentler affections stray back to the broken home. Her smile of parting is very gracious, but it is not after all, such smile as your warm heart pines for.

Ten days after, you are walking toward the old homestead, with such feelings as it never called up before. In the days of boyhood, there were triumphant thoughts of the gladness, and the pride, with which, when grown to the nature of manhood, you would come back to that little town of your birth. As you have bent with your dreamy resolutions over the tasks of the cloister life, swift thoughts have flocked on you of the proud step, and prouder heart, with which you would one day greet the old acquaintances of boyhood; and you have regaled yourself on the jaunty manner with which you would meet old Dr. Bidlow; and the patronizing air, with which you would address the pretty, blue-eyed Madge.

It is late afternoon when you come in sight of the tall sycamores that shade your home; you shudder now lest you may meet any whom you once knew. The first, keen grief of youth seeks little of the sympathy of companions: it lies—with a sensitive man,—bounded within the narrowest circles of the heart. They only who hold the key to its innermost recesses can speak consolation. Years will make a change;—as the summer grows in fierce heat, the balminess of the violet banks of Spring, is lost in the odors of a thousand flowers; —the heart, as it gains in age, loses freshness, but wins breadth.

——Throw a pebble into the brook at its source, and the agitation is terrible, and the ripples chafe madly their narrowed banks;—throw in a pebble, when the brook has become a river, and you see a few circles, widening, and widening, and widening, until they are lost in the gentle, every-day murmur of its life!

A BROKEN HOME.

You draw your hat over your eyes, as you walk toward the familiar door; the yard is silent; the night is falling gloomily; a few katydids are crying in the trees. The mother's window, where—at such a season as this, it was her custom to sit watching your play, is shut; and the blinds are closed over it. The honeysuckle which grew over the window, and which she loved so much, has flung out its branches carelessly; and the spiders have hung their foul nets upon its tendrils.

And she, who made that home so dear to your boyhood,—so real to your after years,—standing amid all the flights of your youthful ambition, and your paltry cares (for they seem paltry now) and your doubts, and anxieties and weaknesses of heart, like the light of your hope—burning ever there, under the shadow of the sycamores,—a holy beacon, by whose guidance you always came to a sweet haven, and to a refuge from all your toils,—is gone, ——gone forever!

The father is there indeed;—beloved, respected, esteemed; but the boyish heart, whose old life is now reviving, leans more readily, and more kindly into that void, where once beat the heart of the mother.

Nelly is there;—cherished now with all the added love that is stricken off from her who has left you forever. Nelly meets you at the door.

——" Clarence!"

——" Nelly!"

There are no other words; but you feel her

tears, as the kiss of welcome is given. With your hand joined in her's, you walk down the hall, into the old, familiar room;—not with the jaunty, college step,—not with any presumption on your dawning manhood,—oh, no,—nothing of this!

Quietly, meekly, feeling your whole heart shattered, and your mind feeble as a boy's, and your purposes nothing, and worse than nothing,—with only one proud feeling, you fling your arm around the form of that gentle sister,—the pride of a protector;—the feeling—"*I* will care for you now, dear Nelly!"—that is all. And even that, proud as it is, brings weakness.

You sit down together upon the lounge; Nelly buries her face in her hands, sobbing.

"Dear Nelly," and your arm clasps her more fondly.

There is a cricket in the corner of the room, chirping very loudly. It seems as if nothing else were living—only Nelly, Clarence, and the noisy cricket. Your eye falls on the chair where she used to sit; it is drawn up with the same care as ever, beside the fire.

"I am *so* glad to see you, Clarence," says Nelly, recovering herself; and there is a sweet, sad smile now. And sitting there beside you, she tells you of it all;—of the day, and of the hour;—and how she looked,—and of her last prayer, and how happy she was.

"And did she leave no message for me, Nelly?"

"Not to forget us, Clarence; but you could not!"

"Thank you, Nelly; and was there nothing else?"

"Yes, Clarence;—to meet her one day!"

You only press her hand.

Presently your father comes in: he greets you with far more than his usual cordiality. He keeps your hand a long time, looking quietly in your face, as if he were reading traces of some resemblance, that had never struck him before.

The father is one of those calm, impassive men, who shows little upon the surface, and whose feelings you have always thought, cold. But now, there is a tremulousness in his tones that you never remember observing before. He seems conscious of it himself, and forbears talking. He goes to his old seat, and after gazing at you a little while with the same steadfastness as at first, leans forward, and buries his face in his hands.

From that very moment, you feel a sympathy, and a love for him, that you have never known till then. And in after years, when suffering or trial come over you, and when your thoughts fly, as to a refuge, to that shattered home, you will recall that stooping image of the father,—with his head bowed, and from time to time trembling convulsively with grief,—and feel that there remains yet by the household fires, a heart of kindred love, and of kindred sorrow.

Nelly steals away from you gently, and stepping across the room, lays her hand upon his shoulder, with a touch, that says, as plainly as words could say it;—"We are here, Father!"

And he rouses himself,—passes his arm around her;—looks in her face fondly,—draws her to him, and prints a kiss upon her forehead.

"Nelly, we must love each other now, more than ever."

Nelly's lips tremble, but she cannot answer; a tear or two go stealing down her cheek.

You approach them; and your father takes your hand again, with a firm grasp,—looks at you thoughtfully,—drops his eyes upon the fire, and for a moment there is a pause;—" We are quite alone, now, my boy!"

-—It is a Broken Home!

VI.

Family Confidence.

GRIEF has a strange power in opening the hearts of those who sorrow in common. The father, who has seemed to you, not so much neglectful, as careless of your aims, and purposes; —toward whom there have been in your younger years, yearnings of affection, which his chilliness of manner has seemed to repress, now grows under the sad light of the broken household, into a friend. The heart feels a joy, it cannot express, in its freedom to love and to cherish. There is a pleasure wholly new to you, in telling him of your youthful projects, in listening to his questionings, in seeking his opinions, and in yielding to his judgment.

It is a sad thing for the child, and quite as sad for the parent, when this confidence is unknown. Many and many a time, with a bursting heart, you have longed to tell him of some boyish grief, or to ask his guidance out of some boyish trouble; but at the first sight of that calm, inflexible face, and at the first sound of his measured words,—your enthusiastic yearnings toward his love, and his counsels, have all turned back upon your eager, and sorrowing heart; and you have gone away to hide in secret, the tears, which the lack of his sympathy has wrung from your soul.

But now, over the tomb of her, for whom you weep in common, there is a new light breaking; and your only fear is, lest you weary him with what may seem a barren show of your confidence.

Nelly, too, is nearer now than ever; and with her, you have no fears of your extravagance; you listen delightfully there, by the evening flame, to all that she tells you of the neighbors of your boyhood. You shudder somewhat at her genial praises of the blue-eyed Madge;—a shudder that you can hardly account for, and which you do not seek to explain. It may be, that there is a clinging and tender memory yet—wakened by the home atmosphere—of the divided sixpence.

Of your quondam friend Frank, the pleasant recollection of whom revives again under the old roof-tree, she tells you very little; and that little in a hesitating, and indifferent way that utterly surprises you. Can it be, you think, that there has been some cause of unkindness?

——Clarence is still very young!

The fire glows warmly upon the accustomed hearth-stone; and—save that vacant place, never to be filled again—a home cheer reigns even in this time of your mourning. The spirit of the lost parent seems to linger over the remnant of the household; and the Bible upon its stand—the book she loved so well—the book so sadly forgotten,—seems still to open on you its promises, in her sweet tones; and to call you, as it were, with her angel voice, to the land that she inherits.

And when late night has come, and the household is quiet, you call up in the darkness of your chamber, that other night of grief, which followed upon the death of Charlie. That was the boy's vision of death; and this is the youthful vision. Yet essentially, there is but little difference. Death levels the capacities of the living, as it levels the strength of its victims. It is as grand to the man, as to the boy: its teachings are as deep for age, as for infancy.

You may learn its manner, and estimate its approaches; but when it comes, it comes always with the same awful front that it wore to your boyhood. Reason and Revelation may point to rich issues that unfold from its very darkness; yet all these are no more to your bodily sense, and no more to your enlightened hope, than those foreshadowings of peace, which rest like a halo, on the spirit of the child, as he prays in guileless tones,—OUR FATHER, WHO ART IN HEAVEN!

It is a holy, and a placid grief that comes over you;—not crushing, but bringing to life from the grave of boyhood, all its better and nobler instincts.

In their light, your wild plans of youth look sadly misshapen; and in the impulse of the hour you abandon them; holy resolutions beam again upon your soul like sunlight; your purposes seem bathed in goodness. There is an effervescence of the spirit, that carries away all foul matter, and leaves you in a state of calm, that seems kindred to the land and to the life, whither the sainted mother has gone.

This calm brings a smile in the middle of tears, and an inward looking, and leaning toward that Eternal Power which governs and guides us;—with that smile and that leaning, sleep comes like an angelic minister, and fondles your wearied frame, and thought, into that repose which is the mirror of the Destroyer.

——Poor Clarence, he is like the rest of the world,—whose goodness lies chiefly in the occasional throbs of a better nature, which soon subside, and leave them upon the old level of *desire*.

As you lie between waking and sleeping, you have a fancy of a sound at your door;—it seems to open softly; and the tall figure of your father wrapped in his dressing-gown stands over you, and gazes—as he gazed at you before;—his look is very mournful; and he murmurs your mother's name; and—sighs; and—looks again; and passes out.

At morning, you cannot tell if it was real, or a dream. Those higher resolves too, which grief, and the night made, seem very vague and shadowy. Life with its ambitious, and cankerous desires wakes again. You do not feel them at first; the subjugation of holy thoughts, and of reaches toward the Infinite, leave their traces on you, and perhaps bewilder you into a half consciousness of strength. But at the first touch of the grosser elements about you;—on your very first entrance upon those duties which quicken pride or shame, and which are pointing at you from every quarter,—your holy calm, your high-born purpose,—your spiritual cleavings pass away, like the electricity of August storms, drawn down by the thousand glittering turrets of a city.

The world is stronger than the night; and the bindings of sense are ten-fold stronger than the most exquisite delirium of soul. This makes you feel, or will one day make you feel, that life,—strong life and sound life,—that life which lends approaches to the Infinite, and takes hold on Heaven, is not so much a PROGRESS, as it is a RESISTANCE.

There is one special confidence, which in all your talk about plans, and purposes, you do not give to your father; you reserve that for the ear of Nelly alone. Why happens it, that a father is almost the last confidant that a son makes in any matter deeply affecting the feelings? Is it the fear that a father may regard such matter as boyish? Is it a lingering suspicion of your own childishness; or of that extreme of affection which reduces you to childishness?

Why is it always, that a man of whatever age or condition, forbears to exhibit to those, whose respect for his judgment, and mental abilities he seeks only, the most earnest qualities of the heart, and those intenser susceptibilities of love, which underlie his nature, and which give a color, in spite of him, to the habit of his life? Why is he so morbidly anxious to keep out of sight any extravagances of affection, when he blurts officiously to the world, his extravagances of action, and of thought? Can any lover explain me this?

Again, why is a sister, the one of all others, to whom you first whisper the dawnings of any strong emotion;—as if it were a weakness, that her charity alone could cover?

However this may be, you have a long story for Nelly's ear. It is some days after your return: you are strolling down a quiet, wooded lane—a remembered place,—when you first open to her your heart. Your talk is of Laura Dalton. You describe her to Nelly, with the extravagance of a glowing hope. You picture those qualities that have attracted you most; you dwell upon her beauty, her elegant figure, her grace of conversation, her accomplishments. You make a study that feeds your passion, as you go on. You rise by the very glow of your speech into a frenzy of feeling, that she has never excited before. You are quite sure that you would be wretched, and miserable, without her.

"Do you mean to marry her?" says Nelly.

It is a question that gives a swift bound to the blood of youth. It involves the idea of possession;

and of the dependence of the cherished one upon your own arm, and strength. But the admiration you entertain, seems almost too lofty for this Nelly's question makes you diffident of reply; and you lose yourself in a new story of those excellencies of speech, and of figure, which have so charmed you.

Nelly's eye, on a sudden, becomes full of tears.
——" What is it, Nelly ? "
" Our mother; Clarence."

The word, and the thought dampen your ardor; the sweet watchfulness, and gentle kindness of that parent, for an instant, make a sad contrast with the showy qualities you have been naming; and the spirit of that mother—called up by Nelly's words —seems to hang over you, with an anxious love, that subdues all your pride of passion.

But this passes; and now,—half believing that Nelly's thoughts have run over the same ground with yours,—you turn special pleader for your fancy. You argue for the beauty, which you just now affirmed; you do your utmost to win over Nelly to some burst of admiration. Yet there she sits beside you, thoughtfully, and half sadly, playing with the frail autumn flowers that grow at her side. What can she be thinking ? You ask it by a look.

She smiles,—takes your hand, for she will not let you grow angry,—

" I was thinking, Clarence, whether this Laura Dalton, would after all, make a good wife,—such an one as you would love always ? "

VII.

A Good Wife.

THE thought of Nelly suggests new dreams, that are little apt to find place in the rhapsodies of a youthful lover. The very epithet of a good wife, mates tamely with the romantic fancies of a first passion. It is measuring the ideal by too practical a standard. It sweeps away all the delightful vagueness of a fairy dream of love, and reduces one to a dull, and economic estimate of actual qualities. Passion lives above all analysis and estimate, and arrives at its conclusions by intuition.

Did Petrarch ever think if Laura would make a good wife; did Oswald ever think it of Corinne? Nay, did even the more practical Waverley, ever think it of the impassioned Flora? Would it not weaken faith in their romantic passages, if you believed it? What have such vulgar, practical issues to do with that passion which sublimates the faculties, and makes the loving dreamer to live in an ideal sphere, where nothing but goodness and brightness can come?

Nelly is to be pitied for entertaining such a thought; and yet Nelly is very good, and kind. Her affections are, without doubt, all centred in the remnant of the shattered home: she has never known any further, and deeper love,—never once fancied it even——

——Ah, Clarence, you are very young!

And yet there are some things that puzzle you in Nelly. You have found, accidentally, in one of her treasured books,—a book that lies almost always on her dressing table,—a little withered flower, with its stem in a slip of paper; and on the paper the initials of—your old friend Frank. You recall, in connection with this, her indisposition to talk of him on the first evening of your return. It seems,—you scarce know why—that these are the tokens of something very like a leaning of the heart. It does occur to you, that she too, may have her little casket of loves; and you try one day, very adroitly, to take a look into this casket.

——You will learn, later in life, that the heart of a modest, gentle girl, is a very hard matter, for even a brother to probe: it is at once the most tender, and the most unapproachable of all fastnesses. It admits feeling, by armies, with great trains of artillery,—but not a single scout. It is as calm and pure as polar snows; but deep underneath, where no footsteps have gone, and where no eye can reach, but one, lies the warm, and the throbbing earth.

Make what you will of the slight, quivering blushes and of the half-broken expressions,—more you cannot get. The love that a delicate-minded girl will tell, is a short-sighted, and outside love; but the love that she cherishes without voice or token, is a love that will mould her secret sympathies, and her deepest, fondest yearnings, either to a quiet world of joy, or to a world of placid sufferance. The true voice of her love she will keep back long and late, fearful ever of her most prized jewel,—fearful to strange sensitiveness: she will show kindness, but the opening of the real floodgates of the heart, and the utterance of those impassioned yearnings, which belong to its nature, come far later. And fearful, thrice fearful is the shock, if these flow out unmet!

That deep, thrilling voice bearing all the perfume of the womanly soul in its flow, rarely finds utterance; and if uttered vainly,—if called out by tempting devices, and by a trust that is abused,— desolate indeed is the maiden heart,—widowed of its chastest thought. The soul shrinks affrighted within itself. Like a tired bird, lost at sea,—fluttering around what seem friendly boughs, it stoops at length, and finding only cold, slippery spars, with no bloom and no foliage—its last hope gone —it sinks to a wild, ocean grave!

Nelly—and the thought brings a tear of sympathy to your eye—must have such a heart: it speaks in every shadow of her action. And this very delicacy seems to lend her a charm, that would make her a wife, to be loved and honored.

Aye, there is something in that maidenly modesty, retiring from you, as you advance,—retreating timidly from all bold approaches, fearful and yet joyous, which wins upon the iron hardness of a man's nature, like a rising flame. To force of action and resolve, he opposes force: to strong will, he mates his own : pride lights pride ; but to the gentleness of the true womanly character, he yields with a gush of tenderness that nothing else can call out. He will never be subjugated on his own ground of action and energy ; but let him be lured to that border country, over which the delicacy, and fondness of a womanly nature presides, and his energy yields, his haughty determination faints,—he is proud of submission.

And with this thought of modesty, and gentleness to illuminate your dream of an ideal wife, you chase the pleasant phantom to that shadowy home, —lying far off in the future,—of which she is the glory, and the crown. I know it is the fashion now-a-days with many to look for a woman's excellencies, and influence,—away from her home ; but I know too, that a vast many eager, and hopeful hearts, still cherish the belief that her virtues will range highest, and live longest within those sacred walls.

Where indeed, can the modest and earnest vir tue of a woman, tell a stronger story of its worth than upon the dawning habit of a child? Where can her grace of character win a higher, and a riper effect, than upon the action of her household? What mean those noisy declaimers who talk of the feeble influence, and of the crushed faculties of a woman?

What school of learning, or of moral endeavor, depends more on its teacher, than the home upon the mother? What influence of all the world's professors, and teachers, tells so strongly on the habit of a man's mind, as those gentle droppings from a mother's lips, which, day by day, and hour by hour, grow into the enlarging stature of his soul, and live with it forever? They can hard'y be mothers, who aim at a broader, and noisier field: they have forgotten to be daughters: they must needs have lost the hope of being wives.

Be this how it may, the heart of a man, with whom affection is not a name, and love a mere passion of the hour, yearns toward the quiet of a home, as toward the goal of his earthly joy, and hope. And as you fasten there, your thought, an indulgent, yet dreamy fancy paints the loved image that is to adorn it, and to make it sacred.

——She is there to bid you—God speed!—and an adieu, that hangs like music on your ear, as you go out to the every-day labor of life. At evening, she is there to greet you, as you come back wearied with a day's toil; and her look so full of gladness, cheats you of your fatigue; and she steals her arm around you with a soul of welcome, that beams like sunshine on her brow, and that fills your eye with tears of a twin gratitude—to her, and Heaven.

She is not unmindful of those old-fashioned virtues of cleanliness, and of order, which give an air of quiet, and which secure content. Your wants are all anticipated; the fire is burning brightly; the clean hearth flashes under the joyous blaze; the old elbow chair is in its place. Your very unworthiness of all this haunts you like an accusing spirit, and yet penetrates your heart with a new devotion, toward the loved one who is thus watchful of your comfort.

She is gentle;—keeping your love, as she has won it, by a thousand nameless and modest virtues, which radiate from her whole life and action. She steals upon your affections like a summer wind breathing softly over sleeping valleys. She gains a mastery over your sterner nature, by very contrast; and wins you unwittingly to her lightest wish. And yet her wishes are guided by that delicate tact, which avoids conflict with your manly pride; she subdues, by seeming to yield. By a single soft word of appeal, she robs your vexation of its anger; and with a slight touch of that fair hand, and one pleading look of that earnest eye, she disarms your sternest pride.

She is kind;—shedding her kindness, as Heaven sheds dew. Who indeed could doubt it?—least of all, you, who are living on her kindness, day by day, as flowers live on light? There is none of that officious parade, which blunts the point of benevolence: but it tempers every action with a blessing. If trouble has come upon you, she knows that her voice beguiling you into cheerfulness, will lay your fears; and as she draws her chair beside you, she knows that the tender and confiding way, with which she takes your hand, and looks up into your earnest face, will drive away from your annoyance all its weight. As she lingers, leading off your thought with pleasant words, she knows well that she is redeeming you from care, and soothing you to that sweet calm, which such home, and such wife can alone bestow. And in sickness,—sickness that you almost covet for the sympathy it brings,—that hand of hers resting on your fevered forehead, or those fingers playing with the scattered locks, are more full of kindness than the loudest vaunt of friends; and when your failing strength will permit no more, you grasp that cherished hand,—with a fullness of joy, of thankfulness, and of love, which your tears only can tell.

She is good;—her hopes live, where the angels live. Her kindness and gentleness are sweetly tempered with that meekness and forbearance which are born of Faith. Trust comes into her heart, as rivers come to the sea. And in the dark hours of doubt and foreboding, you rest fondly upon her buoyant Faith, as the treasure of your common life; and in your holier musings, you look to that frail hand, and that gentle spirit, to lead you away from the vanities of worldly ambition, to the fullness of that joy, which the good inherit.

———Is Laura Dalton, such an one ?

VIII.

A Broken Hope.

YOUTHFUL passion is a giant. It overleaps all the dreams, and all the resolves of our better and quieter nature; and drives madly toward some wild issue, that lives only in its frenzy. How little account does passion take of goodness! It is not within the cycle of its revolution: it is below: it is tamer: it is older: it wears no wings.

And your proud heart flashing back to the memory of that sparkling eye, which lighted your hope—full-fed upon the vanities of cloister learning, drives your soberer visions to the wind. As you recall those tones, so full of brilliancy and pride, the quiet virtues fade, like the soft haze upon a spring landscape, driven westward by a swift, sea-born storm. The pulse bounds: the eyes flash: the heart trembles with its sharp springs. Hope dilates, like the eye,—fed with swift blood, leaping to the brain.

Again the image of Miss Dalton, so fine, so noble, so womanly, fills, and bounds the Future. The lingering tears of grief drop away from your eye, as the lingering loves of boyhood drop from your scalding passion, or drift into clouds of vapor.

You listen to the calm, thoughtful advice of the father, with a deep consciousness of something stronger than his counsels, seething in your bosom. The words of caution, of instruction, of guidance, fall upon your heated imagination, like the night-dews upon the crater of an Etna. They are beneficent, and healthful for the straggling herbage upon the surface of the mountain; but they do not reach, or temper the inner fires, that are rolling their billows of flame, beneath.

You drop hints from time to time to those with whom you are most familiar, of some prospective change of condition. There is a new and cheerful interest in the building plans of your neighbors:—a new, and cheerful study of the principles of domestic architecture;—in which, very elegant boudoirs, adorned with harps, hold prominent place; and libraries with gilt-bound books, very rich in lyrical, and dramatic poetry;—fine views from bay windows;—graceful pots of flowers;—sleek-looking Italian grey-hounds;—cheerful sunlight;—musical goldfinches chattering on the wall;—superb pictures of Princesses in peasant dresses;—soft Axminster carpets;—easy-acting bell-pulls;—gigantic candelabras;—porcelain vases of classic shape;—neat waiters in white aprons;—luxurious lounges; and, to crown them all with the very height of your pride,—the elegant Laura, the mistress, and the guardian of your soul—moving amid the scene, like a new Duchess of Vallière!

You catch chance sights here and there, of the blue-eyed Madge: you see her, in her mother's household, the earnest, and devoted daughter,—gliding gracefully about her mother's cottage, the very type of gentleness, and of duty. Yet withal, there are sparks of spirit in her, that pique your pride,—lofty as it is. You offer flowers, which she accepts with a kind smile;—not of coquetry—but of simplest thankfulness. She is not the girl to gratify your vanity with any half-show of tenderness. And if there lived ever in her heart an old girlish liking for the school-boy Clarence, it is all gone before the romantic lover of the elegant Laura; or at most, it lies in some obscure corner of her soul, never to be brought to light.

You enter upon the new pursuits, which your father has advised, with a lofty consciousness,—not only of the strength of your mind, but of your heart. You relieve your opening professional study, with long letters to Miss Dalton, full of Shakspearean compliments, and touched off with very dainty elaboration. And you receive pleasant, gossipping notes in answer,—full of quotations, but meaning very little.

Youth is in a grand flush, like the hot days of

ending summer; and pleasant dreams thrall your spirit, like the smoky atmosphere that bathes the landscape of an August day. Hope rides high in the Heavens, as when the summer sun mounts nearest to the zenith. Youth feels the fullness of maturity, before the second season of life is ended: yet is it a vain maturity, and all the glow is deceitful. Those fruits that ripen in summer do not last. They are sweet; they are glowing with gold; but they melt with a luscious softness upon the lip. They do not give that strength, and nutriment, which will bear a man bravely through the coming chills of winter.

The last scene of summer changes now to the cobwebbed ceiling of an attorney's office. Books of law, scattered ingloriously at your elbow, speak dully to the flush of your vanities. You are seated at your side desk, where you have wrought at those heavy, mechanic labors of drafting, which go before a knowledge of your craft.

A letter is by you, which you regard with strange feelings: it is yet unopened. It comes from Laura. It is in reply to one which has cost you very much of exquisite elaboration. You have made your avowal of feeling, as much like a poem, as your education would admit. Indeed, it was a pretty letter,—promising, not so much the trustful love of an earnest, and devoted heart,—as the fervor of a passion which consumed you, and glowed like a furnace through the lines of your letter. It was a confession, in which your vanity of intellect had taken very entertaining part; and in which, your judgment was too cool to appear at all.

She must needs break out into raptures at such a letter; and her own, will doubtless be tempered with even greater passion.

It is well to shift your chair somewhat, so that the clerks of the office may not see your emotion as you read. It would be silly to manifest your exuberance in a dismal, dark office of your instructing attorney. One sighs rather for woods, and brooks, and sunshine, in whose company, the hopes of youth stretch into fulfillment.

We will look only at a closing passage :—

———" My friend Clarence will I trust believe me, when I say that his letter was a surprise to me. To say that it was very grateful, would be what my womanly vanity could not fail to claim. I only wish that I was equal to the flattering portrait which he has drawn. I even half fancy that he is joking me, and can hardly believe that my matronly air should have quite won his youthful heart. At least I shall try not to believe it; and when I welcome him one day, the husband of some fairy, who is worthy of his love, we will smile together at the old lady, who once played the Circe to his senses. Seriously, my friend Clarence, I know your impulse of heart has carried you away: and that in a year's time, you will smile with me, at your old penchant for one so much your senior, and so ill-suited to your years, as your true friend,

LAURA."

——Magnificent Miss Dalton !
Read it again. Stick your knife in the desk :— tut !—you will break the blade ! Fold up the letter carefully, and toss it upon your pile of papers. Open Chitty again ;—pleasant reading is Chitty ! Lean upon your hand—your two hands ;—so that no one will catch sight of your face. Chitty is very interesting ; — how sparkling and imaginative — what a depth and flow of passion in Chitty !

The office is a capital place—so quiet and sunny. Law is a delightful study—so captivating, and such stores of romance ! And then those trips to the Hall offer such relief and variety ;—especially just now. It would be well not to betray your eagerness to go. You can brush your hat a round or two, and take a peep into the broken bit of looking-glass, over the wash-stand.

You lengthen your walk, as you sometimes do, by a stroll upon the Battery—though rarely, upon such a blustering November day. You put your hands in your pockets, and look out upon the tossing sea.

It is a fine sight—very fine. There are few finer bays in the world than New York bay ; either to look at, or—for that matter—to sleep in. The ships ride up thickly, dashing about the cold spray delightfully ; the little cutters gleam in the November sunshine, like white flowers shivering in the wind.

The sky is rich—all mottled with cold, gray streaks of cloud. The old apple-women, with their noses frost-bitten, look cheerful, and blue. The ragged immigrants in short-trowsers, and bell-crowned hats, stalk about with a very happy expression, and very short stemmed pipes; their yellow-haired babies look comfortably red, and glowing. And the trees with their scant, pinched foliage, have a charming, summer-like effect!

Amid it all, the thoughts of the boudoir, and harpsichord, and goldfinches, and Axminster carpets, and sunshine, and Laura, are so very—very pleasant! How delighted you would be to see her married to the stout man in the red cravat, who gave her bouquets, and strolled with her on the deck of the steamer upon the St. Lawrence! What a jaunty, self-satisfied air he wore; and with what considerate forbearance he treated you—calling you once or twice—Master Clarence! It never occurred to you before, how much you must be indebted to that pleasant, stout man.

You try sadly to be cheerful; you smile oddly; your pride comes strongly to your help, but yet helps you very little. It is not so much a broken heart, that you have to mourn over, as a broken dream. You seem to see in a hundred ways that had never occurred to you before, the marks of her superior age. Above all, it is manifest in the cool, and unimpassioned tone of her letter. Yet, how kindly, withal! It would be a relief to be angry.

New visions come to you, wakened by the broken fancy which has just now eluded your grasp. You will make yourself, if not old,—at least, gifted with the force and dignity of age. You will be a man; and build no more castles, until you can people them with men. In an excess of pride, you even take umbrage at the sex; they can have little appreciation of that engrossing tenderness, of which you feel yourself to be capable. Love shall henceforth be dead, and you will live boldly without it.

——Just so, when some dark, eastern cloud-bank shrouds for a morning, the sun of later August, we say in our shivering pride—the winter is come early! But God manages the seasons better than we; and in a day, or an hour perhaps, the cloud will pass, and the heavens glow again upon our ungrateful heads.

Well, it is even so, that the passionate dreams of youth break up, and wither. Vanity becomes tempered with wholesome pride; and passion yields to the riper judgment of manhood;—even as the August heats pass on, and over, into the genial glow of a September sun. There is a strong growth in the struggles against mortified pride; and then only, does the youth get an ennobling consciousness of that manhood which is dawning in him, when he has fairly surmounted those puny vexations, which a wounded vanity creates.

Now, your heart is driven home;—and that

cherished place, where, so little while ago, you wore your vanities with an air, that mocked even your grief, and that subdued your better nature, seems to stretch toward you, over long miles of distance,—its wings of love, and to welcome back to the sister's, and the father's heart—not the self-sufficient, and vaunting youth,—but the brother and son,—the school-boy, Clarence. Like a thirsty child, you stray in thought, to that fountain of cheer; and live again,—your vanity crushed, your wild hope broken,—in the warm, and natural affections of the boyish home.

Clouds weave the SUMMER into the season of AUTUMN: and YOUTH rises from dashed hopes, into the stature of a MAN.

Autumn;

OR,

THE DREAMS OF MANHOOD.

DREAMS OF MANHOOD.

Autumn.

THERE are those who shudder at the approach of Autumn; and who feel a light grief stealing over their spirits, like an October haze, as the evening shadows slant sooner, and longer, over the face of an ending August day.

But is not Autumn the Manhood of the year? Is it not the ripest of the seasons? Do not proud flowers blossom;—the golden rod, the orchis, the dahlia, and the bloody cardinal of the swamplands?

The fruits too are golden, hanging heavy from the tasked trees. The fields of maize show weeping spindles, and broad rustling leaves, and ears, half glowing with the crowded corn; the September wind whistles over their thick-set ranks, with whispers of plenty. The staggering stalks of the buck-wheat grow red with ripeness; and tip their tops with clustering, tri-cornered kernels.

The cattle loosed from the summer's yoke, grow strong upon the meadows, new starting from the scythe. The lambs of April, rounded into fullness of limb, and gaining day by day their woolly cloak, bite at the nodding clover-heads; or, with their noses to the ground, they stand in solemn, circular conclave, under the pasture oaks, while the noon sun beats with the lingering passion of July.

The Bob-o'-Lincolns have come back from their Southern rambles among the rice, all speckled with gray; and—singing no longer as they did in Spring,—they quietly feed upon the ripened reeds, that straggle along the borders of the walls. The larks, with their black and yellow breast-plates, and lifted heads, stand tall upon the close-mown meadow; and at your first motion of approach, spring up, and soar away, and light again; and with their lifted heads, renew the watch. The quails, in half-grown coveys, saunter hidden, through the underbrush that skirts the wood; and only when you are close upon them, whir away, and drop scattered under the coverts of the forest.

The robins, long ago deserting the garden neighborhood, feed at eventide, in flocks, upon the bloody berries of the sumac; and the soft-eyed pigeons dispute possession of the feast. The squirrels chatter at sun-rise, and gnaw off the full-grown burs of the chesnuts. The lazy black-birds skip after the loitering cow watchful of the crickets, that her slow steps start to danger. The crows, in companies, caw aloft; and hang high over the carcase of some slaughtered sheep, lying ragged upon the hills.

The ash trees grow crimson in color, and lose their summer life in great gouts of blood. The birches touch their frail spray with yellow; the chesnuts drop down their leaves in brown, twirling showers. The beeches crimped with the frost, guard their foliage, until each leaf whistles white, in the November gales. The bitter-sweet hangs its bare, and leaf-less tendrils from rock to tree, and sways with the weight of its brazen berries. The sturdy oaks, unyielding to the winds, and to the frosts, struggle long against the approaches of the winter; and in their struggles, wear faces of orange, of scarlet, of crimson, and of brown; and finally, yielding to swift winds,—as youth's pride yields to manly duty,—strew the ground with the scattered glories of their summer strength; and warm, and feed the earth, with the debris of their leafy honors.

The maple, in the low-lands, turns suddenly its silvery greenness into orange scarlet; and in the coming chilliness of the Autumn eventide, seems to catch the glories of the sunset; and to wear them as a sign of God's old promise in Egypt,—like a pillar of cloud, by day,—and of fire, by night.

And when all these are done;—and in the paved, and noisy aisles of the city, the ailanthus, with all its greenness gone,—lifts up its skeleton fingers to the God of Autumn and of storms,—the dog-wood still guards its crown; and the branches which stretched their white canvas in April, now bear up a spire of bloody tongues, that lie against the leafless woods, like a tree on fire.

Autumn brings to the home, the cheerful glow of "first fires." It withdraws the thoughts from the wide and joyous landscape of summer, and fixes them upon those objects which bloom, and rejoice within the household. The old hearth that has rioted the summer through with boughs and blossoms, gives up its withered tenantry. The firedogs gleam kindly upon the evening hours; and the blaze wakens those sweet hopes, and prayers, which cluster around the fireside of home.

The wanton and the riot of the season gone, are softened in memory, and supply joys to the season to come;—just as youth's audacity and pride, give a glow to the recollections of our manhood.

At mid-day, the air is mild and soft; a warm, blue smoke lies in the mountain gaps; the tracery of distant woods upon the upland, hangs in the haze, with a dreamy gorgeousness of coloring. The river runs low with August drought; and frets upon the pebbly bottom, with a soft, low murmur, —as of joyousness gone by. The hemlocks of the river bank, rise in tapering sheens, and tell tales of Spring.

As the sun sinks, doubling his disc in the October smoke, the low, south wind creeps over the withered tree-tops, and drips the leaves upon the land. The windows that were wide open at noon, are closed; and a bright blaze—to drive off the Eastern dampness, that promises a storm,—flashes lightly, and kindly, over the book-shelves and busts, upon my wall.

As the sun sinks lower, and lower, his red beams die in a sea of great, gray clouds. Slowly, and quietly, they creep up over the night-sky. Venus is shrouded. The Western stars blink faintly,— then fade in the mounting vapors. The vane points East of South. The constellations in the Zenith, struggle to be seen;—but presently give over, and hide their shining.

By late lamp-light, the sky is all gray and dark : the vane has turned two points nearer East. The clouds spit fine rain-drops, that you only feel, with your face turned to the heavens. But soon, they grow thicker and heavier; and, as I sit, watching the blaze, and——dreaming,——they patter thick and fast under the driving wind, upon the window,—like the swift tread of an army of **MEN** !

I.

Pride of Manliness.

AND has manhood no dreams? Does the soul wither at that Rubicon, which lies between the Gallic country of youth, and the Rome of manliness? Does not fancy still love to cheat the heart, and weave gorgeous tissues to hang upon that horizon, which lies along the years that are to come? Is happiness so exhausted, that no new forms of it lie in the mines of imagination, for busy hopes to drag up to-day?

Where then would live the motives to an upward looking of the eye, and of the soul;—where, the beckonings that bid us ever—onward?

But these later dreams, are not the dreams of fond boyhood, whose eye sees rarely below the surface of things; nor yet the delicious hopes of sparkling blooded youth: they are dreams of sober trustfulness, of practical results, of hard-wrought world success, and—may be—of Love and of Joy.

Ambitious forays do not rest, where they rested once: hitherto, the balance of youth has given you, in all that you have dreamed of accomplishment,— a strong vantage against age: hitherto, in all your estimates, you have been able to multiply them by that access of thought, and of strength, which manhood would bring to you. Now, this is forever ended.

There is a great meaning in that word—manhood. It covers all human growth. It supposes no extensions, or increase; it is integral, fixed, perfect—the whole. There is no getting beyond manhood; it is much to give up to it; but once reached, you are all that a man was made to be, in this world.

It is a strong thought—that a man is perfected, so far as strength goes;—that he will never be abler to do his work, than under the very sun which is now shining on him. There is a seriousness, that few call to mind, in the reflection, that whatever you do in this age of manhood, is an unalterable type of your whole bigness. You may qualify particulars of your character, by refinements, by special studies, and practice; but,— once a man,—and there is no more manliness to be lived for.

This thought kindles your soul to new, and swifter dreams of ambition than belong to youth. They were toys; these are weapons. They were fancies; these are motives. The soul begins to struggle with the dust, the sloth, the circumstance, that beleaguer humanity, and to stagger into the van of action.

Perception, whose limits lay along a narrow horizon, now tops that horizon, and spreads, and reaches toward the heaven of the Infinite. The mind feels its birth, and struggles toward the great birth-master. The heart glows: its humanities even, yield and crimple under the fierce heat of mental pride. Vows leap upward, and pile rampart upon rampart, to scale all the degrees of human power.

Are there not times in every man's life when there flashes on him a feeling—nay, more, an absolute conviction,—that this soul is but a spark belonging to some upper fire; and that by as much as we draw near by effort, by resolve, by intensity of endeavor, to that upper fire,—by so much, we draw nearer to our home, and mate ourselves with angels? Is there not a ringing desire in many minds to seize hold of what floats above us in the universe of thought, and drag down what shreds we can, to scatter to the world? Is it not belonging to greatness, to catch lightning, from the plains where lightning lives, and curb it, for the handling of men?

Resolve is what makes a man manliest;—not puny resolve, not crude determination, not errant purpose,—but that strong, and indefatigable will, which treads down difficulties and danger, as a boy treads down the heaving frost-lands of winter;—which kindles his eye and brain, with a proud pulse-beat toward the unattainable. Will makes men giants. It made Napoleon an Emperor of kings,—Bacon a fathomer of nature,—Byron a tutor of passion, and the martyrs, masters of Death.

In this age of manhood, you look back upon the dreams of the years that are past; they glide to the vision in pompous procession; they seem bloated with infancy. They are without sinew or bone. They do not bear the hard touches of the man's hand.

It is not long, to be sure, since the summer of life ended with that broken hope; but the few years that lie between have given long steps upward. The little grief that threw its shadow, and the broken vision that deluded you, have made the passing years long, in such feeling as ripens manhood. Nothing lays the brown of autumn upon the green of summer, so quick as storms.

There have been changes too in the home scenes; these graft age upon a man. Nelly—your sweet Nelly of childhood, your affectionate sister of youth, has grown out of the old brotherly companionship into the new dignity of a household.

The fire flames and flashes upon the accustomed hearth. The father's chair is there in the wonted corner; he himself—we must call him the old man now, though his head shows few white honors—wears a calmness and a trust that light the failing eye. Nelly is not away; Nelly is a wife; and the husband yonder, as you may have dreamed,—your old friend Frank.

Her eye is joyous; her kindness to you is unabated; her care for you is quicker and wiser. But yet the old unity of the household seems broken; nor can all her winning attentions bring back the feeling which lived in Spring, under the garret roof.

The isolation, the unity, the integrity of manhood, make a strong prop for the mind; but a weak one for the heart. Dignity can but poorly fill up that chasm of the soul, which the home affections once occupied. Life's duties, and honors press hard upon the bosom, that once throbbed at a mother's tones, and that bounded in a mother's smiles.

In such home, the strength you boast of, seems a weakness; manhood leans into childish memories, and melts—as Autumn frosts yield to a soft, south wind, coming from a Tropic spring. You feel in a desert where you once felt at home—in a bounded landscape,—that was once—the world.

The tall sycamores have dwindled to paltry trees; the hills that were so large, and lay at such grand distance to the eye of childhood, are now near by, and have fallen away to mere rolling waves of upland. The garden fence that was so gigantic, is now only a simple paling: its gate that was such a cumbrous affair—reminding you of Gaza—you might easily lift from its hinges. The lofty dovecote, which seemed to rise like a monument of art, before your boyish vision, is now only a flimsy box upon a tall spar of hemlock.

The garret even, with its lofty beams, its dark stains, and its obscure corners, where the white hats, and coats hung ghost-like, is but a low loft, darkened by age,—hung over with cobwebs, dimly lighted with foul windows,—its romping Charlie, —its glee,—its swing,—its joy,—its mystery, all gone forever.

The old gallipots, and retorts are not anywhere to be seen in the second story window of the brick school. Dr. Bidlow is no more! The trees that seemed so large, the gymnastic feats that were so extraordinary, the boy that made a snapper of his handkerchief,—have all lost their greatness, and their dread. Even the springy usher, who dressed his hair with the ferule, has become the middle-aged father of five curly-headed boys, and has entered upon what once seemed the gigantic commerce—of 'stationery and account books.'

The marvellous labyrinth of closets, at the old mansion where you once paid a visit—in a coach— is all dissipated. They have turned out to be the merest cupboards in the wall. Nat, who had travelled, and seen London, is by no means so surprising a fellow to your manhood, as he was to the boy. He has grown spare, and wears spectacles. He is not so famous as he was. You would hardly think of consulting him now about your marriage; or even about the price of goats upon London bridge.

As for Jenny--your first, fond flame!—lively romantic, black-eyed Jenny,—the reader of Thaddeus of Warsaw,—who sighed and wore blue ribbons on her bonnet,—who wrote love notes,—who talked so tenderly of broken hearts,—who used a glass seal with a cupid and a dart,—dear Jenny,—she is now the plump, and thriving wife of the apothecary of the town! She sweeps out every morning at seven, the little entry of the apothecary's house: she buys a 'joint' twice a week from the butcher, and is particular to have the 'knuckle' thrown in, for soups: she wears a sky blue calico gown, and dresses her hair in three little flat quirls on either side of her head—each one pierced through with a two-pronged hair-pin.

She does not read Thaddeus of Warsaw, now.

II.

Man of the World.

FEW persons live through the first periods of manhood, without strong temptations to be counted—'men of the world.' The idea looms grandly among those vanities, that hedge a man's approach to maturity.

Clarence is in good training for the acceptance of this idea. The broken hope which clouded his closing youth, shoots over its influence upon the dawn of manhood. Mortified pride had taught—as it always teaches—not caution only, but doubt, distrust, indifference. A new pride grows up on the ruins of the old, weak, and vain pride of youth. Then, it was a pride of learning, or of affection; now, it is a pride of indifference. Then, the world proved bleak, and cold, as contrasted with his shining dreams; and now, he accepts the proof, and wins from it what he can.

The man of the world puts on the method, and

measure of the world: he studies its humors. He gives up the boyish notion of a sincerity among men, like that of youth: he lives, to seem. He conquers such annoyances as the world may thrust upon him, in the shape of grief, or losses, like a practised athlete of the ring. He studies moral sparring.

With somewhat of this strange vanity growing on you, you do not suffer the heart to wake into life, except in such fanciful dreams as tempt you back to the sunny slopes of childhood.

In this mood, you fall in with Dalton, who has just returned from a year passed in the French Capital. There is an easy suavity, and graceful indifference in his manner that chimes admirably with your humor. He is gracious without needing to be kind. He is a friend, without any challenge or proffer of sincerity. He is an adept in those world tactics, which match him with all men, but which link him to none. He has made it his art to be desired, and admired, but rarely to be trusted. You could not have a better teacher.

Under such instruction, you become disgusted for the time, with any effort, or pulse of affection, which does not have immediate and practical bearing upon the success in life, by which you measure your hopes. The dreams of love, of romantic adventure, of placid joy have all gone out, with the fantastic images, to which your passionate youth had joined them. The world is now regarded as a tournament, where the gladiatorship of life is to be exhibited at your best endeavor. Its honors and joy, lie in a brilliant pennant, and a plaudit.

Dalton is learned in those arts which make of action—not a duty, but a conquest; and sense of duty has expired in you, with those romantic hopes, to which you bound it,—not as much through sympathy, as ignorance. It is a cold, and a bitterly selfish work that lies before you,—to be covered over with such borrowed show of smiles, as men call affability. The heart wears a stout, brazen screen ; its inclinations grow to the habit of your ambitious projects.

In such mood come swift dreams of wealth ;— not of mere accumulation, but of the splendor, and parade, which in our western world are, alas its chiefest attractions. You grow observant of markets, and estimate per centages. You fondle some speculation in your thought, until it grows into a gigantic scheme of profit; and if the venture prove successful, you follow the tide tremulously, until some sudden reverse throws you back upon the resources of your professional employ.

But again as you see this and that one wearing the blazonry which wealth wins, and which the man of the world is sure to covet—your weak soul glows again with the impassioned desire; and you hunger, with brute appetite, and bestial eye—for riches. You see the mania around you; and it is relieved of odium, by the community of error. You consult some gray old veteran in the war of gold, scarred with wounds, and crowned with honors, and watch eagerly for the words and the ways, which have won him wealth.

Your fingers tingle with mad expectancies; your eyes roam—lost in estimates. Your note-book shows long lines of figures. Your reading of the news centres in the stock list. Your brow grows cramped with the fever of anxiety. Through whole church hours, your dreams range over the shadowy transactions of the week or the month to come.

Even with old religious habit clinging fast to your soul, you dream now, only of nice conformity, comfortable faith, high respectability; there lies very little in you of that noble consciousness of Duty performed,—of living up to the Life that is in you,—of grasping boldly and stoutly, at those chains of Love which the Infinite Power has lowered to our reach. You do not dream of being, but of seeming. You spill the real essence, and clutch at the vial which has only a label of Truth. Great and holy thoughts of the Future,—shadowy, yet bold conceptions of the Infinite, float past you dimly, and your hold is never strong enough to grapple them to you. They fly like eagles, too near the sun; and there lies game below, for your vulture beak to feed upon.

[Great thoughts belong, only and truly, to him whose mind can hold them. No matter who first puts them in words; if they come to a soul, and fill it, they belong to it;—whether they floated on the voice of others; or on the wings of silence, and the night.]

To be up with the fashion of the time,—to be ignorant of plain things and people, and to be knowing in brilliancies, is a kind of Pelhamism, that is very apt to overtake one in the first blush of manhood. To hold a fair place in the after-dinner table-talk, to meet distinction as a familiarity, to wear salon honors with aplomb, to know affection so far as to wield it into grace of language, are all splendid achievements with a man of the world. Instruction is caught, without asking it; and no ignorance so shames, as ignorance of those forms, by which natural impulse is subdued to the tone of civilian habit. You conceal what tells of the man; and cover it with what smacks of the roué.

Perhaps, under such training, and with a slight memory of early mortification to point your spirit, you affect those gallantries of heart and action, which the world calls flirtation. You may study brilliancies of speech, to wrap their net around those susceptible hearts, whose habit is too naïve by nature, to wear the leaden covering of custom. You win approaches by artful counterfeit of earnestness; and dash away any *naïveté* of confidence with some brave sophism of the world. A doubt or a distrust, piques your pride, and makes attentions wear humility that wins anew. An indifference piques you more, and throws into your art counter indifference,—lit up by bold flashes of feeling,—sparkling with careless brilliancies, and crowned with a triumph of neglect.

It is curious how ingeniously a man's vanity

will frame apologies for such actions.——It is pleasant to give pleasure; you like to see a joyous sparkle of the eye, whether lit up by your presence, or by some buoyant fancy. It is a beguiling task to weave words into some soft, melodious flow, that shall keep the ear, and kindle the eye;—and to strew it over with half-hidden praises, so deftly couched in double terms, that their aroma shall only come to the heart hours afterward; and seem to be the merest accidents of truth. It is a happy art to make such subdued show of emotion, as seems to struggle with pride; and to flush the eye with a moisture, of which you seem ashamed, and yet are proud. It is a pretty practice, to throw an earnestness into look and gesture, that shall seem full of pleading, and yet—ask nothing!

And yet it is hard to admire greatly the reputation of that man, who builds his triumphs upon womanly weakness: that distinction is not over enduring, whose chiefest merit springs out of the delusions of a too trustful heart. The man who wins it, wins only a poor sort of womanly distinction. Without power to cope with men, he triumphs over the weakness of the other sex, only by hypocrisy. He wears none of the armor of Romans; and he parleys with Punic faith.

——Yet, even now,—there is a lurking goodness in you, that traces its beginnings to the old garret home;—there is an air in the harvest heats, that whispers of the bloom of spring.

And over your brilliant career as man of

the world,—however lit up by a morbid vanity, or galvanized by a lascivious passion, there will come at times, the consciousness of a better heart struggling beneath your cankered action,—like the low Vesuvian fire, reeking vainly under rough beds of tufa, and scoriated lava. And as you smile in loge, or salon, with daring smiles; or press with villian fondness, the hand of those lady votaries of the same god you serve, there will gleam upon you, over the waste of rolling years, a memory that quickens again the nobler, and bolder instincts of the heart.

Childish recollections, with their purity, and earnestness,—a sister's love,—a mother's solicitude, will flood your soul once more with a gushing sensibility that yearns for enjoyment. And the consciousness of some lingering nobility of affection, that can only grow great in mating itself with nobility of heart, will sweep off your puny triumphs, your Platonic friendships, your dashing coquetries, —like the foul smoke of a city, before a fresh breeze of the country autumn.

III.

Manly Hope.

YOU are at home again;—not your own home, that is gone; but at the home of Nelly, and of Frank. The city heats of summer drive you to the country. You ramble, with a little kindling of old desires and memories, over the hill sides that once bounded your boyish vision. Here you netted the wild rabbits, as they came out at dusk, to feed; there, upon that tall chesnut, you cruelly maimed your first captive squirrel. The old maples are even now scarred with the rude cuts you gave them, in sappy March.

You sit down upon some height, overlooking the valley where you were born; you trace the faint silvery line of river; you detect by the leaning elm, your old bathing place upon the Saturdays of Summer. Your eye dwells upon some patches of pasture wood, which were famous for their nuts. Your rambling, and saddened vision roams over the houses; it traces the familiar chimney-stacks; it searches out the low-lying cottages; it dwells upon the gray roof, sleeping yonder under the sycamores.

Tears swell in your eye, as you gaze; you cannot tell whence, or why they come. Yet they are tears eloquent of feeling. They speak of brother children—of boyish glee—of the flush of young health,—of a mother's devotion,—of the home affections,—of the vanities of life,—of the wasting years, of the Death that must shroud what friends remain, as it has shrouded what friends have gone,—and of that GREAT HOPE, beaming on your seared manhood dimly, from the upper world.

Your wealth suffices for all the luxuries of life: there is no fear of coming want; health beats strong in your veins; you have learned to hold a place in the world, with a man's strength, and a man's confidence. And yet in the view of those sweet scenes which belonged to early days, when neither strength, confidence, nor wealth were yours, days never to come again,—a shade of melancholy broods upon your spirit; and covers with its veil all that fierce pride which your worldly wisdom has wrought.

You visit again, with Frank, the country homestead of his grandfather; he is dead; but the old lady still lives; and blind Fanny, now drawing toward womanhood, wears yet through her darkened life, the same air of placid content, and of sweet trustfulness in Heaven. The boys whom you astounded with your stories of books are gone, building up now with steady industry the queen cities of our new Western land. The old clergyman is gone from the desk, and from under his sounding board; he sleeps beneath a brown stone slab in the church yard. The stout deacon is dead; his wig and his wickedness rest together. The tall chorister sings yet: but they have now a bass viol—handled by a new schoolmaster, in place of his tuning fork; and the years have sown feeble quavers in his voice.

Once more you meet at the home of Nelly,—the blue eyed Madge. The sixpence is all forgotten; you cannot tell where your half of it is gone. Yet she is beautiful—just budding into the full ripeness of womanhood. Her eyes have a quiet, still joy, and hope beaming in them, like angel's looks. Her motions have a native grace, and freedom, that no culture can bestow. Her words have a gentle earnestness and honesty, that could never nurture guile.

You had thought, after your gay experiences of the world, to meet her with a kind condescension, as an old friend of Nelly's. But there is that in her eye, which forbids all thought of condescension. There is that in her air, which tells of a high womanly dignity, which can only be met on equal ground. Your pride is piqued. She has known—she must know your history; but it does not tame her. There is no marked and submissive appreciation of your gifts, as a man of the world.

She meets your happiest compliments with a very easy indifference; she receives your elegant civilities with a very assured brow. She neither courts your society, nor avoids it. She does not seek to provoke any special attention. And only when your old-self glows in some casual kindness to Nelly, does her look beam with a flush of sympathy.

This look touches you. It makes you ponder on the noble heart that lives in Madge. It makes you wish it were yours. But that is gone. The fervor and the honesty of a glowing youth, is swallowed up in the flash and splendor of the world. A half-regret chases over you at night-fall, when solitude pierces you with the swift dart of gone-by memories. But at morning, the regret dies, in the glitter of ambitious purposes.

The summer months linger; and still you linger with them. Madge is often with Nelly; and Madge is never less than Madge. You venture to point your attentions with a little more fervor; but she meets the fervor with no glow. She knows too well the habit of your life.

Strange feelings come over you;—feelings like half-forgotten memories—musical—dreamy—doubtful. You have seen a hundred faces more brilliant than that of Madge; you have pressed a hundred jewelled hands that have returned a half-pressure to yours. You do not exactly admire;—to love, you have forgotten;—you only—linger!

It is a soft autumn evening, and the harvest moon is red and round over the eastern skirt of woods. You are attending Madge to that little cottage home, where lives that gentle and doting mother, who in the midst of comparative poverty, cherishes that refined delicacy which never comes to a child, but by inheritance.

Madge has been passing the day with Nelly. Something—it may be the soft autumn air wafting toward you the freshness of young days,—moves you to speak, as you have not ventured to speak,—as your vanity has not allowed you to speak before.

"You remember, Madge, (you have guarded this sole token of boyish intimacy) our split sixpence?"

"Perfectly:" it is a short word to speak, and there is no tremor in her tone—not the slightest.

"You have it yet?"

"I dare say, I have it somewhere:" no tremor now: she is very composed.

"That was a happy time:" very great emphasis on the word happy

"Very happy:"—no emphasis anywhere.

"I sometimes wish I might live it over again."

"Yes?"—inquiringly.

"There are after all no pleasures in the world like those."

"No?"—inquiringly again.

You thought you had learned to have language at command: you never thought, after so many years schooling of the world, that your pliant tongue would play you truant. Yet now,—you are silent.

The moon steals silvery into the light flakes of cloud, and the air is soft as May. The cottage is in sight. Again you risk utterance:—

"You must live very happily here."

"I have very kind friends:"—the very, is emphasized.

"I am sure Nelly loves you very much."

"Oh, I believe it!"—with great earnestness.

You are at the cottage door:—

"Good night, Maggie,"—very feelingly.

"Good night, Clarence,"—very kindly; and she draws her hand coyly, and half tremulously from your somewhat fevered grasp.

You stroll away dreamily—watching the moon,—running over your fragmentary life;—half moody,—half pleased,—half hopeful.

You come back stealthily, and with a heart throbbing with a certain wild sense of shame, to watch the light gleaming in the cottage. You linger in the shadows of the trees, until you catch a glimpse of her figure, gliding past the window. You bear the image home with you. You are silent on your return. You retire early;—but you do not sleep early.

——If you were only as you were:—if it were not too late! If Madge could only love you, as you know she will, and must love one manly heart, there would be a world of joy opening before you.

You draw out Nelly to speak of Madge: Nelly is very prudent. "Madge is a dear girl,"—she says. Does Nelly even distrust you? It is a sad thing to be too much a man of the world.

You go back again to noisy, ambitious life: you try to drown old memories in its blaze, and its vanities. Your lot seems cast, beyond all change; and you task yourself with its noisy fulfilment. But amid the silence, and the toil of your office hours, a strange desire broods over your spirit;— a desire for more of manliness,—that manliness which feels itself a protector of loving, and trustful innocence.

You look around upon the faces in which you have smiled unmeaning smiles:—there is nothing there to feed your dawning desires. You meet with those ready to court you by flattering your vanity—by retailing the praises of what you may do well,—by odious familiarity,—by brazen proffer of friendship; but you see in it only the emptiness, and the vanity, which you have studied to enjoy.

Sickness comes over you, and binds you for weary days and nights;—in which life hovers doubtfully, and the lips babble secrets that you cherish. It is astonishing how disease clips a man from the artificialities of the world. Lying lonely upon his bed, moaning, writhing, suffering, his soul joins on to the universe of souls by only natural bonds. The factitious ties of wealth, of place, of reputation, vanish from his bleared eyes; and the earnest heart, deep under all, craves only—heartiness.

The old yearning of the office silence comes back;

—not with the proud wish only—of being a protector, but—of being protected. And whatever may be the trust in that beneficent Power, who 'chasteneth whom he loveth,'—there is yet an earnest, human leaning toward some one, whose love—most, and whose duty—least, would call her to your side;—whose soft hands would cool the fever of yours,—whose step would wake a throb of joy,—whose voice would tie you to life, and whose presence would make the worst of Death—an Adieu!

As you gain strength once more, you go back to Nelly's home. Her kindness does not falter; every care and attention belong to you there. Again your eye rests upon that figure of Madge, and upon her face, wearing an even gentler expression, as she sees you sitting pale and feeble by the old hearthstone. She brings flowers—for Nelly: you beg Nelly to place them upon the little table at your side. It is as yet the only taste of the country that you can enjoy. You love those flowers.

After a time you grow strong, and walk in the fields. You linger until nightfall. You pass by the cottage where Madge lives. It is your pleasantest walk. The trees are greenest in that direction; the shadows are softest; the flowers are thickest.

It is strange—this feeling in you. It is not the feeling you had for Laura Dalton. It does not even remind of that. That was an impulse; but this is growth. That was strong; but this is—strength. You catch sight of her little notes to

Nelly; you read them over and over; you treasure them; you learn them by heart. There is something in the very writing, that touches you.

You bid her adieu with tones of kindness that tremble;—and that meet a half-trembling tone in reply. She is very good.

——If it were not too late!

IV.

Manly Love.

AND shall pride yield at length? ——Pride!——and what has love to do with pride? Let us see how it is.

Madge is poor; she is humble. You are rich; you are a man of the world; you are met respectfully by the veterans of fashion; you have gained perhaps a kind of brilliancy of position.

Would it then be a condescension to love Madge? Dare you ask yourself such a question? Do you not know,—in spite of your worldliness,—that the man or the woman who *condescends* to love never loves in earnest?

But again, Madge is possessed of a purity, a delicacy, and a dignity that lift her far above you,—that make you feel your weakness, and your unworthiness; and it is the deep, and the mortifying sense of this unworthiness, that makes you bolster yourself upon your pride. You *know* that you do yourself honor, in loving such grace and goodness; —you know that you would be honored tenfold more than you deserve, in being loved—by so much grace, and goodness.

It scarce seems to you possible; it is a joy too great to be hoped for: and in the doubt of its attainment, your old, worldly vanity comes in, and tells you to—beware; and to live on, in the splendor of your dissipation, and in the lusts of your selfish habit. Yet still, underneath all, there is a deep, low, heart-voice,—quickened from above,— which assures you that you are capable of better things;—that you are not wholly lost; that a mine of unstarted tenderness still lies smouldering in your soul.

And with this sense quickening your better nature, you venture the wealth of your whole heart-life, upon the hope that now blazes on your path.

——You are seated at your desk, working with such zeal of labor, as your ambitious projects never could command. It is a letter to Margaret Boyne, that so tasks your love, and makes the veins upon your forehead swell with the earnestness of the employ.

——" DEAR MADGE—May I not call you thus, if only in memory of our childish affections;—and might I dare to hope that a riper affection which your character has awakened, may permit me to call you thus, always?

"If I have not ventured to speak, dear Madge, will you not believe that the consciousness of my own ill-desert has tied my tongue;—will you not, at least, give me credit for a little remaining modesty of heart? You know my life, and you know my character—what a sad jumble of errors, and of misfortunes have belonged to each. You know the careless, and the vain purposes which have made me recreant to the better nature, which belonged to that sunny childhood, when we lived, and grew up—together. And will you not believe me when I say, that your grace of character, and kindness of heart, have drawn me back from the follies in which I lived; and quickened new desires, which I thought to be wholly dead? Can I indeed hope that you will overlook all that has gained your secret reproaches; and confide in a heart, which is made conscious of better things, by the love—you have inspired?

"Ah, Madge, it is not with a vain show of words, or with any counterfeit of feeling, that I write now;—you know it is not;—you know that my heart is leaning toward you, with the freshness of its noblest instincts;—you know that—I love you!

"Can I, dare I hope, that it is not spoken in vain? I had thought in my pride, never to make such avowal,—never again to sue for affection; but your gentleness, your modesty, your virtues of life and heart, have conquered me. I am sure you will treat me with the generosity of a victor.

"You know my weaknesses;—I would not conceal from you a single one,—even to win you. I can offer nothing to you, which will bear comparison in value, with what is yours to bestow. I can only offer this feeble hand of mine—to guard you; and this poor heart to love you!

"Am I rash? Am I extravagant, in word, or in hope? Forgive it then, dear Madge, for the sake of our old childish affection; and believe me, when I say, that what is here written,—is written honestly, and tearfully.   Adieu."

It is with no fervor of boyish passion, that you fold this letter: it is with the trembling hand of eager, and earnest manhood. They tell you that man is not capable of love;—so, the September sun is not capable of warmth. It may not indeed be so fierce as that of July; but it is steadier. It does not force great flaunting leaves into breadth and succulence; but it matures whole harvests of plenty.

There is a deep and earnest soul pervading the reply of Madge that makes it sacred, it is full of delicacy, and full of hope. Yet it is not final. Her heart lies entrenched within the ramparts of Duty and of Devotion. It is a citadel of strength, in the middle of the city of her affections. To win the way to it, there must be not only earnestness of love, but earnestness of life.

Weeks roll by; and other letters pass and are answered,—a glow of warmth beaming on either side.

You are again at the home of Nelly; she is very joyous; she is the confidant of Madge. Nelly feels, that with all your errors, you have enough inner goodness of heart to make Madge happy; and she feels—doubly—that Madge has such excess of goodness as will cover your heart with joy. Yet she tells you very little. She will give you no full assurance of the love of Madge; she leaves that for yourself to win.

She will even tease you in her pleasant way, until hope almost changes to despair; and your brow grows pale with the dread—that even now, your unworthiness may condemn you.

It is summer weather; and you have been walking over the hills of home with Madge, and Nelly. Nelly has found some excuse to leave you,—glancing at you most teazingly, as she hurries away.

You are left sitting with Madge, upon a bank tufted with blue violets. You have been talking of the days of childhood, and some word has called up the old chain of boyish feeling, and joined it to your new hope.

What you would say, crowds too fast for utterance; and you abandon it. But you take from your pocket that little, broken bit of sixpence,—which you have found after long search,—and without a word, but with a look that tells your inmost thought, you lay it in the half-opened hand of Madge.

She looks at you, with a slight suffusion of color,—seems to hesitate a moment,—raises her other hand, and draws from her bosom, by a bit of blue ribbon, a little locket. She touches a spring, and there falls beside your relique,—another, that had once belonged to it.

Hope glows now like the sun.

―――" And you have worn this, Maggie?"

―――" Always!"

" Dear Madge!"

" Dear Clarence!"

―――And you pass your arm now, unchecked, around that yielding, graceful figure; and fold her to your bosom, with the swift, and blessed assurance, that your fullest, and noblest dream of love is won.

V.

Cheer and Children.

WHAT a glow there is to the sun! What warmth—yet it does not oppress you; what coolness—yet it is not too cool. The birds sing sweetly; you catch yourself watching to see what new songsters they can be:—they are only the old robins and thrushes;—yet what a new melody is in their throats!

The clouds hang gorgeous shapes upon the sky,—shapes they could hardly ever have fashioned before. The grass was never so green, the buttercups were never so plenty; there was never such a life in the leaves. It seems as if the joyousness in you, gave a throb to nature, that made every green thing buoyant.

Faces too are changed: men look pleasantly: children are all charming children: even babies look tender and lovable. The street beggar at your door is suddenly grown into a Belisarius, and is one of the most deserving heroes of modern times. Your mind is in a continued ferment; you glide through your toil—dashing out sparkles of passion—like a ship in the sea. No difficulty daunts you: there is a kind of buoyancy in your soul, that rocks over danger or doubt, as sea-waves heave calmly and smoothly, over sunken rocks.

You grow unusually amiable and kind; you are earnest in your search of friends; you shake hands with your office boy, as if he were your second cousin. You joke cheerfully with the stout washer-woman; and give her a shilling over-change, and insist upon her keeping it; and grow quite merry at the recollection of it. You tap your hackman on the shoulder very familiarly, and tell him he is a capital fellow; and don't allow him to whip his horses, except when driving to the post-office. You even ask him to take a glass of beer with you, upon some chilly evening. You drink to the health of his wife.—He says he has no wife:—whereupon you think him a very miserable man; and give him a dollar, by way of consolation.

You think all the editorials in the morning papers are remarkably well-written,—whether upon your side, or upon the other. You think the stock-market has a very cheerful look,—even with Erie—of which you are a large holder—down to seventy-five. You wonder why you never admired Mrs. Hemans before, or Stoddart, or any of the rest.

You give a pleasant twirl to your fingers, as you saunter along the street; and say—but not so loud as to be overheard—" She is mine—she is mine!"

You wonder if Frank ever loved Nelly, one half as much as you love Madge?—You feel quite sure he never did. You can hardly conceive how it is, that Madge has not been seized before now, by scores of enamored men, and borne off, like the Sabine women in Romish history. You chuckle over your future, like a boy who has found a guinea, in groping for sixpences. You read over the marriage service,—thinking of the time when you will take *her* hand, and slip the ring upon *her* finger; and repeat after the clergyman—'for richer —for poorer; for better—for worse.' A great deal of 'worse' there will be about it, you think!

Through all, your heart cleaves to that sweet image of the beloved Madge, as light cleaves to day. The weeks leap with a bound; and the months only grow long, when you approach that day which is to make her yours. There are no flowers rare enough to make bouquets for her; diamonds are too dim for her to wear; pearls are tame.

——And after marriage, the weeks are even shorter than before: you wonder why on earth all the single men in the world, do not rush tumultuously to the Altar; you look upon them all, as a travelled man will look upon some conceited Dutch boor, who has never been beyond the limits of his cabbage-garden. Married men, on the contrary, you regard as fellow-voyagers; and look upon their wives—ugly as they may be—as, better than none.

You blush a little, at first telling your butcher what 'your wife' would like; you bargain with the grocer for sugars and teas, and wonder if he *knows* that you are a married man? You practise your new way of talk upon your office boy;—you tell him that 'your wife' expects you home to dinner; and are astonished that he does not stare to hear you say it.

You wonder if the people in the omnibus know, that Madge and you are just married; and if the driver knows, that the shilling you hand to him, is for 'self and wife?' You wonder if any body was ever so happy before, or ever will be so happy again?

You enter your name upon the hotel books as 'Clarence —— and Lady'; and come back to look at it,—wondering if any body else has noticed it,—and thinking that it looks remarkably well. You cannot help thinking that every third man you meet in the hall, wishes he possessed your wife;—nor do you think it very sinful in him, to wish it. You fear it is placing temptation in the way of covetous men, to put Madge's little gaiters outside the chamber door, at night.

Your home, when it is entered, is just what it should be:—quiet, small, with everything she wishes, and nothing more than she wishes. The sun strikes it in the happiest possible way:—the piano is the sweetest-toned in the world;—the library is stocked to a charm;—and Madge, that blessed wife, is there,—adorning, and giving life to it all. To think, even, of her possible death, is a suffering you class with the infernal tortures of the Inquisition. You grow twain of heart, and of purpose. Smiles seem made for marriage; and you wonder how you ever wore them before.

So, a year and more wears off, of mingled home-life, visiting, and travel. A new hope and joy lightens home :—there is a child there.

——What a joy to be a father! What new emotions crowd the eye with tears, and make the hand tremble! What a benevolence radiates from you toward the nurse,—toward the physician—toward everybody! What a holiness, and sanctity of love grows upon your old devotion to that wife of your bosom,—the mother of your child!

The excess of joy seems almost to blur the stories of happiness which attach to heaven. You are now joined, as you were never joined before, to the great family of man. Your name and blood will live after you; nor do you once think (what father can?) but that it will live honorably and well.

With what a new air you walk the streets! With what a triumph, you speak in your letter to Nelly,—of 'your family!' Who, that has not felt it, knows what it is—to be 'a man of family!

How weak now, seem all the imaginations of your single life: what bare, dry skeletons of the reality, they furnished! You pity the poor fellows who have no wives or children,—from your soul you count their smiles, as empty smiles, put on to cover the lack that is in them. There is a free-masonry among fathers, that they know nothing of. You compassionate them deeply: you think them worthy objects of some charitable association: you would cheerfully buy tracts for them, if they would but read them,—tracts on marriage and children.

——And then ' the boy '——*such* a boy!

There was a time, when you thought all babies very much alike:——alike? Is your boy like anything, except the wonderful fellow that he is? Was there ever a baby seen, or even read of, like that baby?

——Look at him:—pick him up in his long, white gown: he may have an excess of color,—but such a pretty color! he is a little pouty about the mouth—but such a mouth! His hair *is* a little scant, and he is rather wandering in the eye;—but, Good Heavens,—what an eye!

There was a time, when you thought it was very absurd for fathers to talk about their children; but it does not seem at all absurd now. You think, on the contrary, that your old friends, who used to sup with you at the club, would be delighted to know how your baby is getting on, and how much he measures around the calf of the leg! If they pay you a visit, you are quite sure they are in an agony to see Frank; and you hold the little squirming fellow in your arms, half conscience-smitten, for provoking them to such envy, as they must be suffering. You make a settlement upon the boy with a chuckle,—as if you were treating yourself to a mint-julep,—instead of conveying away a few thousands of seven per cents.

——Then the boy developes, astonishingly. What a head—what a foot,—what a voice! And he is so quiet withal;—never known to cry, except under such provocation as would draw tears from a heart of adamant; in short, for the first six months, he is never anything, but gentle, patient, earnest, loving, intellectual, and magnanimous. You are half afraid that some of the physicians will be reporting the case, as one of the most remarkable instances of perfect moral and physical development, on record.

But the years roll on, in the which your extravagant fancies, die into the earnest maturity of a father's love. You struggle gaily with the cares that life brings to your door. You feel the strength of three beings in your single arm; and feel your heart warming toward God and man, with the added warmth of two other loving, and trustful beings.

How eagerly you watch the first tottering step of that boy: how you riot in the joy and pride, that swell in that mother's eyes, as they follow his feeble, staggering motions! Can God bless his creatures, more than he has blessed that dear Madge, and you? Has Heaven even richer joys, than live in that home of yours?

By and by, he speaks; and minds tie together by language, as the hearts have long tied by looks. He wanders with you, feebly, and with slow, wondering paces, upon the verge of the great universe of thought. His little eye sparkles with some vague fancy that comes upon him first, by language. Madge teaches him the words of affection, and of thankfulness; and she teaches him to lisp infant prayer; and by secret pains, (how could she be so secret?) instructs him in some little phrase of endearment, that she knows will touch your heart; and then, she watches your coming; and the little fellow runs toward you, and warbles out his lesson of love, in tones that forbid you any answer,—save only those brimming eyes,—turned first on her, and then on him;—and poorly concealed by the quick embrace, and the kisses which you shower in transport!

Still slip on the years, like brimming bowls of nectar. Another Madge is sister to Frank; and a little Nelly, is younger sister to this other Madge.

——Three of them—a charmed, and mystic number;—which if it be broken in these young days,—as, alas, it may be!—will only yield a cherub angel, to float over you, and to float over them—to wean you, and to wean them, from this world, where all joys perish, to that seraph world, where joys last forever.

VI.

A Dream of Darkness.

IS our life a sun, that it should radiate light and heat forever? Do not the calmest, and brightest days of autumn, show clouds that drift their ragged edges over the golden disc; and bear down swift, with their weight of vapors, until the whole sun's surface is shrouded;—and you can see no shadow of tree, or flower upon the land, because of the greater, and gulphing shadow of the cloud?

Will not life bear me out;—will not truth, earnest and stern, around me, make good the terrible imagination that now comes swooping heavily, and darkly, upon my brain?

You are living in a little village, not far away from the city. It is a graceful, and luxurious home that you possess. The holly and the laurel gladden its lawn in winter; and bowers of blossoms sweeten it through all the summer. You know, each day of your return from the town, where first you will catch sight of that graceful figure, flitting like a shadow of love, beneath the trees : you know well, where you will meet the joyous, and noisy welcome of stout Frank, and of tottling Nelly. Day after day, and week after week, they fail not.

A friend sometimes attends you ; and a friend to you, is always a friend to Madge. In the city, you fall in once more with your old acquaintance Dalton ;—the graceful, winning, yet dissolute man that his youth promised. He wishes to see your cottage home. Your heart half hesitates : yet it seems folly to cherish distrust of a boon companion, in so many of your revels.

Madge receives him with that sweet smile, which welcomes all your friends. He gains the heart of Frank, by talking of his toys, and of his pigeons ; and he wins upon the tenderness of the mother, by his attentions to the child. Even you, repent of your passing shadow of dislike, and feel your heart warming toward him, as he takes little Nelly in his arms, and provokes her joyous prattle.

Madge is unbounded in her admiration of your friend : he renews, at your solicitation, his visit : he proves kinder than ever ; and you grow ashamed of your distrust.

Madge is not learned in the arts of a city life : the accomplishments of a man of the world are almost new to her : she listens with eagerness to Dalton's graphic stories of foreign fêtes, and lux-

try: she is charmed with his clear, bold voice, and with his manly execution of little operatic airs.

——She is beautiful—that wife who has made your heart whole, by its division—fearfully beautiful. And she is not cold, or impassive: her heart though fond, and earnest, is yet human:—we are all human. The accomplishments and graces of the world must needs take hold upon her fancy. And a fear creeps over you, that you dare not whisper,—that those graces may cast into the shade, your own yearning, and silent tenderness.

But this is a selfish fear, that you think you have no right to cherish. She takes pleasure in the society of Dalton,—what right have you, to say her—nay? His character indeed is not altogether such as you could wish; but will it not be selfish to tell her even this? Will it not be even worse, and show taint of a lurking suspicion, which you know would wound her grievously? You struggle with your distrust, by meeting him more kindly than ever: yet, at times, there will steal over you a sadness,—which that dear Madge detects, and sorrowing in her turn, tries to draw away from you by the touching kindness of sympathy. Her look, and manner kill all your doubt; and you show that it is gone, and piously conceal the cause, by welcoming in gayer tones than ever, the man who has fostered it, by his presence.

Business calls you away to a great distance from home: it is the first long parting of your real manhood. And can suspicion, or a fear, lurk amid

those tearful embraces? Not one,——thank God,
—not one!

Your letters, frequent and earnest, bespeak your increased devotion ; and the embraces you bid her give to the sweet ones of your little flock, tell of the calmness, and sufficiency of your love. Her letters too, are running over with affection :—what though she mentions the frequent visits of Dalton, and tells stories of his kindness and attachment? You feel safe in her strength : and yet—yet there is a brooding terror that rises out of your knowledge of Dalton's character.

And can you tell her this; can you stab her fondness, now that you are away, with even a hint of what would crush her delicate nature?

What you know to be love, and what you fancy to be duty, struggle long : but love conquers. And with sweet trust in her, and double trust in God, you await your return. That return will be speedier than you think.

You receive one day a letter : it is addressed in the hand of a friend, who is often at the cottage, but who has rarely written to you. What can have tempted him now? Has any harm come near your home? No wonder your hands tremble at the opening of that sheet ;——no wonder that your eyes run like lightning over the hurried lines. Yet there is little in them—very little. The hand is stout and fair. It is a calm letter,—a friendly letter ; but it is short—terribly short. It bids you come home—'*at once!*'

——And you go. It is a pleasant country you have to travel through; but you see very little of the country. It is a dangerous voyage perhaps, you have to make; but you think very little of the danger. The creaking of the timbers, and the lashing of the waves, are quieting music, compared with the storm of your raging fears. All the while, you associate Dalton with the terror that seems to hang over you; and yet,—your trust in Madge, is true as Heaven!

At length you approach that home;—there lies your cottage lying sweetly upon its hill-side; and the autumn winds are soft; and the maple-tops sway gracefully, all clothed in the scarlet of their frost-dress. Once again, as the sun sinks behind the mountain with a trail of glory, and the violet haze tints the grey clouds, like so many robes of angels,—you take heart and courage; and with firm reliance on the Providence that fashions all forms of beauty, whether in Heaven or in heart,—your fears spread out, and vanish with the waning twilight.

She is not at the cottage door to meet you; she does not expect you; and yet your bosom heaves, and your breathing is quick. Your friend meets you, and shakes your hand.——" Clarence," he says, with the tenderness of an old friend,—" be a man!"

Alas, you are a man;—with a man's heart, and a man's fear, and a man's agony! Little Frank comes bounding toward you joyously—yet under traces of tears:—" Oh, Papa, Mother is gone!"

——" Gone! "——And you turn to the face of your friend;—it is well he is near by, or you would have fallen.

He can tell you very little; he has known the character of Dalton; he has seen with fear his assiduous attentions—tenfold multiplied since your leave. He has trembled for the issue: this very morning he observed a travelling carriage at the door;—they drove away together. You have no strength to question him. You see that he fears the worst:—he does not know Madge, so well as you.

——And can it be? Are you indeed widowed with that most terrible of widowhoods?—Is your wife living,—and yet—lost! Talk not to such a man of the woes of sickness, of poverty, of death; —he will laugh at your mimicry of grief.

——All is blackness; whichever way you turn it is the same; there is no light; your eye is put out; your soul is desolate forever. The heart, by which you had grown up into the full stature of joy, and blessing, is rooted out of you, and thrown like something loathsome, at which the carrion dogs of the world scent, and snuffle!

They will point at you, as the man who has lost all that he prized; and she has stolen it, whom he prized more than what was stolen. And he, the accursed miscreant —— But no, it can never be. Madge is as true as Heaven!

Yet she is not there: whence comes the light that is to cheer you?

——Your children?

Aye, your children,—your little Nelly,—your noble Frank,—they are yours;—doubly, trebly tenfold yours, now that she, their mother, is a mother no more to them, forever!

Aye, close your doors; shut out the world;— draw close your curtains;—fold them to your heart,—your crushed, bleeding, desolate heart. Lay your forehead to the soft cheek of your noble boy;—beware, beware how you dampen that damask cheek with your scalding tears:—yet you cannot help it;—they fall—great drops,—a river of tears, as you gather him convulsively to your bosom!

"Father, why do you cry so?" says Frank, with the tears of dreadful sympathy starting from those eyes of childhood.

——"Why, Papa?"—mimes little Nelly.

——Answer them if you dare! Try it;—what words—blundering, weak words,—choked with agony,—leading no where,—ending in new, and convulsive clasps of your weeping, motherless children.

Had she gone to her grave, there would have been a holy joy—a great, and swelling grief indeed, —but your poor heart would have found a rest in the quiet churchyard; and your feelings rooted in that cherished grave, would have stretched up toward Heaven their delicate leaves, and caught the dews of His grace, who watcheth the lilies. But now,—with your heart cast under foot, or buffeted on the lips of a lying world,—finding no shelter, and no abiding place——alas, we do guess at infinitude, only by suffering.

——Madge, Madge! can this be so? Are you not still the same, sweet, guileless child of Heaven!

VII.

Peace.

IT is a dream;—fearful to be sure,—but only a dream. Madge *is* true. That soul is honest; it could not be otherwise. God never made it to be false; He never made the sun for darkness.

And before the evening has waned to midnght, sweet day has broken on your gloom;—Madge is folded to your bosom;—sobbing fearfully;—not for guilt, or any shadow of guilt, but for the agony she reads upon your brow, and in your low sighs.

The mystery is all cleared by a few lightning words, from her indignant lips; and her whole figure trembles, as she shrinks within your embrace, with the thought of that great evil, that seemed to shadow you. The villain has sought by every art to beguile her into appearance which should compromise her character, and so wound her delicacy, as to take away the courage for return: he has even wrought upon her affection for you, as his master-weapon: a skilfully-contrived story of some accident that had befallen you, had wrought upon her—to the sudden, and silent leave of home. But he has failed. At the first suspicion of his falsity, her dignity and virtue shivered all his malice. She shudders at the bare thought of that fiendish scheme, which has so lately broken on her view.

"Oh, Clarence, Clarence, could you for one moment believe this of me?"

"Dear Madge, forgive me, if a dreamy horror did for an instant palsy my better thought;—it is gone utterly;—it will never—never come again!"

And there she leans, with her head pillowed on your shoulder, the same sweet angel, that has led you in the way of light; and who is still your blessing, and your pride.

He—and you forbear to name his name—is gone;—flying vainly from the consciousness of guilt, with the curse of Cain upon him,—hastening toward the day, when Satan shall clutch his own.

A heavenly peace descends upon you that night;—all the more sacred and calm, for the fearful agony that has gone before. A Heaven that seemed lost, is yours. A love that you had almost doubted, is beyond all suspicion. A heart that in the madness of your frenzy, you had dared to question, you worship now, with blushes of shame. You thank God, for this great goodness, as you never thanked him for any earthly blessing before; and with this twin gratitude lying on your hearts, and clearing your face to smiles, you live on together the old life of joy, and of affection.

Again with brimming nectar, the years fill up their vases. Your children grow into the same earnest joyousness, and with the same home faith, which lightened upon your young dreams; and toward which, you seem to go back, as you riot with them in their Christmas joys, or upon the velvety lawn of June.

Anxieties indeed overtake you; but they are those anxieties which only the selfish would avoid —anxieties that better the heart, with a great weight of tenderness. It may be, that your mischievous Frank runs wild with the swift blood of boyhood, and that the hours are long, which wait his coming. It may be that your heart echoes in silence, the mother's sobs, as she watches his fits of waywardness, and showers on his very neglect, excess of love.

Danger perhaps creeps upon little, joyous Nelly, which makes you tremble for her life; the mother's tears are checked that she may not deepen your grief; and her care guards the little sufferer, like a Providence. The nights hang long and heavy; dull, stifled breathing wakes the chamber with ominous sound; the mother's eye scarce closes, but rests with fond sadness upon the little struggling victim of sickness; her hand rests like an angel touch upon the brow, all beaded with the heats of fever; the straggling, gray light of morning breaks through the crevices of the closed blinds,—bringing stir, and bustle to the world, but, in your home,—lighting only the darkness.

Hope sinking in the mother's heart, takes hold on Faith in God; and her prayer, and her placid look of submission,—more than all your philosophy,—add strength to your faltering courage.

But little Nelly brightens; her faded features take on bloom again; she knows you; she presses your hand; she draws down your cheek to her parched lip; she kisses you, and smiles. The mother's brow loses its shadow; day dawns within, as well as without; and on bended knees, God is thanked!

Perhaps poverty faces you;—your darling schemes break down. One by one, with failing heart, you strip the luxuries from life. But the sorrow which oppresses you, is not the selfish sorrow which the lone man feels; it is far nobler; its chiefest mourning is over the despoiled home. Frank must give up his promised travel; Madge must lose her favorite pony; Nelly must be denied her little fête upon the lawn. The home itself, endeared by so many scenes of happiness, and by so many of suffering—must be given up. It is hard—very hard to tear away your wife, from the flowers, the birds, the luxuries, that she has made so dear.

Now, she is far stronger than you. She contrives new joys; she wears a holy calm; she cheers by a new hopefulness; she buries even the memory of luxury, in the riches of the humble home, that her wealth of heart endows. Her soul, catching radiance from that Heavenly world, where her hope lives, kindles amid the growing shadows, and sheds balm upon the little griefs,—like the serene moon, slanting the dead sun's life, upon the night.

Courage wakes in the presence of those dependent on your toil. Love arms your hand, and quickens your brain. Resolutions break large from the swelling soul. Energy leaps into your action. like night. Gradually you bring back into your humble home, a few traces of the luxury that once adorned it. That wife whom it is your greatest pleasure to win to smiles,—wears a half sad look, as she meets these proofs of love; she fears that you are perilling too much, for her pleasure.

——For the first time in life you deceive her. You have won wealth again; you now step firmly upon your new-gained sandals of gold. But you conceal it from her. You contrive a little scheme of surprise, with Frank alone, in the secret.

You purchase again the old home; you stock it, as far as may be, with the old luxuries; a new harp is in the place of that one which beguiled so many hours of joy; new and cherished flowers bloom again upon the window; her birds hang, and warble their melody, where they warbled it before. A pony—like as possible to the old—is there for Madge; a fête is secretly contrived upon the lawn. You even place the old, familiar books, upon the parlor table.

The birth-day of your own Madge, is approaching:—a fête you never pass by, without home-rejoicings. You drive over with her, upon that morning, for another look at the old place; a cloud touches her brow,—but she yields to your wish. An old servant,—whom you had known in better days—throws open the gates.

——"It is too—too sad," says Madge—"let us go back, Clarence, to our own home;—we are happy there."

——"A little farther, Madge."

The wife steps slowly over what seems the sepulchre of so many pleasures; the children gambol as of old, and pick flowers. But the mother checks them.

"They are not ours now, my children!"

You stroll to the very door; the goldfinches are hanging upon the wall; the mignonette is in the window. You feel the hand of Madge trembling upon your arm; she is struggling with her weakness.

A tidy waiting woman shows you into the old parlor:——there is a harp; and there too, such books as we loved to read.

Madge is overcome; now, she entreats:—"Let us go away, Clarence!" and she hides her face.

——"Never, dear Madge, never! it is yours—all yours!"

She looks up in your face; she sees your look of triumph; she catches sight of Frank bursting in at the old hall-door, all radiant with joy.

----" Frank! — Clarence!" — the tears forbid any more.

"God bless you, Madge! God bless you!"

And thus, in peace and in joy, MANHOOD passes on into the third season of our life—even as golden AUTUMN, sinks slowly into the tomb of WINTER.

Winter;

OR,

THE DREAMS OF AGE.

DREAMS OF AGE.

Winter.

SLOWLY, thickly, fastly, fall the snow flakes,—like the seasons upon the life of man. At the first, they lose themselves in the brown mat of herbage, or gently melt, as they fall upon the broad stepping stone at the door. But as hour after hour passes, the feathery flakes stretch their white cloak plainly on the meadow, and chilling the doorstep with their multitude, cover it with a mat of pearl.

The dried grass tips pierce the mantle of white, like so many serried spears; but as the storm goes softly on, they sink one by one to their snowy tomb; and presently show nothing of all their army, save one or two straggling banners of blackened and shrunken daisies.

Across the white meadow that stretches from my window, I can see nothing of those hills which were so green in summer: between me and them, lie only the soft, slow moving masses, filling the air with whiteness. I catch only a glimpse of one gaunt, and bare-armed oak, looming through the feathery multitude, like a tall ship's spars breaking through fog.

The roof of the barn is covered; and the leaking eaves show dark stains of water, that trickle down the weather-beaten boards. The pear-trees that wore such weight of greenness in the leafy June, now stretch their bare arms to the snowy blast, and carry upon each tiny bough, a narrow burden of winter.

The old house dog marches stately through the strange covering of earth, and seems to ponder on the welcome he will show,—and shakes the flakes from his long ears, and with a vain snap at a floating feather, he stalks again to his dry covert in the shed. The lambs that belonged to the meadow flock, with their feeding ground all covered, seem to wonder at their losses; but take courage from the quiet air of the veteran sheep, and gambol after them, as they move sedately toward the shelter of the barn.

The cat, driven from the kitchen door, beats a coy retreat, with long reaches of her foot, upon the yielding surface. The matronly hens saunter out, at a little lifting of the storm; and eye curiously, with heads half turned, their sinking steps; and then fall back with a quiet cluck of satisfaction, to the wholesome gravel by the stable door.

By and by, the snow flakes pile more leisurely

they grow large and scattered, and come more
slowly than before. The hills that were brown,
heave into sight,—great, rounded billows of white.
The gray woods look shrunken to half their height,
and stand wading in the storm. The wind fresh
ens, and scatters the light flakes that crown the
burden of the snow; and as the day droops, a
clear, bright sky of steel color cleaves the land,
and clouds, and sends down a chilling wind to
bank the walls, and to freeze the storm. The moon
rises full and round, and plays with a joyous chill,
over the glistening raiment of the land.

I pile my fire with the clean cleft hickory; and
musing over some sweet story of the olden time, I
wander into a rich realm of thought, until my eyes
grow dim, and dreaming of battle and of prince, I
fall to sleep in my old farm chamber.

At morning, I find my dreams all written on
the window, in crystals of fairy shape. The cattle, one by one, with ears frost-tipped, and with
frosted noses, wend their way to the watering-place
in the meadow. One by one they drink, and crop
at the stunted herbage, which the warm spring
keeps green and bare.

A hound bays in the distance; the smoke of
cottages rises straight toward Heaven; a lazy
jingle of sleigh-bells wakens the quiet of the high-
road; and upon the hills, the leafless woods stand
low, like crouching armies, with guns and spears
in rest; and among them, the scattered spiral
pines rise like banner-men, uttering with their

thousand tongues of green, the proud war-cry. 'God is with us!'

But, the sky of winter is as capricious as the sky of spring—even as the old wander in thought, like the vagaries of a boy.

Before noon, the heavens are mantled with a leaden gray; the eaves that leaked in the glow of the sun, now tell their tale of morning's warmth, in crystal ranks of icicles. The cattle seek their shelter; the few, lingering leaves of the white oaks, rustle dismally; the pines breathe sighs of mourning. As the night darkens, and deepens the storm, the house dog bays; the children crouch in the wide chimney corners; the sleety rain comes in sharp gusts. And, as I sit by the light leaping blaze in my chamber, the scattered hail-drops beat upon my window, like the tappings of an OLD MAN's cane.

I.

What is Gone.

GONE! Did it ever strike you, my reader, how much meaning lies in that little monosyllable—gone?

Say it to yourself at nightfall, when the sun has sunk under the hills, and the crickets chirp—'gone.' Say it to yourself, when the night is far over, and you wake with some sudden start, from pleasant dreams,—'gone.' Say it to yourself in some country church-yard, where your father, or your mother, sleeps under the blooming violets of spring—'gone.' Say it, in your sobbing prayer to Heaven, as you cling lovingly, but oh, how vainly, to the hand of your sweet wife—'gone!'

Aye, is there not meaning in it? And now, what is gone;—or rather, what is not gone? Childhood is gone with all its blushes, and fairness,—with all its health and wanton,—with all its smiles, like glimpses of heaven; and all its tears, which were but the suffusion of joy.

Youth is gone;—bright, hopeful youth, when you counted the years with jewelled numbers, and hung lamps of ambition at your path, which lighted the palace of renown;—when the days were woven into weeks of blithe labor, and the weeks were rolled into harvest months of triumph, and the months were bound into golden sheaves of years—all, gone!

The strength and pride of manhood is gone; your heart and soul have stamped their deepest dye; the time of power is past; your manliness has told its tale; henceforth your career is *down;*—— hitherto, you have journeyed *up*. You look back upon a decade, as you once looked upon a half score of months; a year has become to your slackened memory, and to your dull perceptions, like a week of childhood. Suddenly and swiftly, come past you, great whirls of gone-by thought, and wrecks of vain labor, eddying upon the stream that rushes to the grave. The sweeping outlines of life, that lay once before the vision—rolling into wide billows of years, like easy lifts of a broad mountain-range,—now seem close-packed together, as with a Titan band; and you see only crowded, craggy heights, — like Alpine fastnesses, — parted with glaciers of grief, and leaking abundant tears.

Your friends are gone;—they who counselled and advised you, and who protected your weakness, will guard it no more forever. One by one they have dropped away as you have journeyed on and yet your journey does not seem a long one

Life, at the longest, is but a bubble that bursts, so soon as it is rounded.

Nelly, your sweet sister, to whom your heart clung so fondly in the young days, and to whom it has clung ever since, in the strongest bonds of companionship,—is gone,—with the rest.

Your thought,—wayward now, and flickering,—runs over the old days with quick, and fevered step; it brings back, faintly as it may, the noisy joys, and the safety, that belonged to the old garret roof; it figures again the image of that calm-faced father,—long since sleeping beside your mother; it rests like a shadow, upon the night when Charlie died, it grasps the old figures of the school-room, and kindles again (how strange is memory) the fire that shed its lustre upon the curtain, and the ceiling, as you lay groaning with your first hours of sickness.

Your flitting recollection brings back with gushes of exultation, the figure of that little, blue-eyed hoyden,—Madge,—as she came with her work, to pass the long evenings with Nelly; it calls again the shy glances that you cast upon her, and your naïve ignorance of all the little counter-play, that might well have passed between Frank and Nelly. Your mother's form too, clear and distinct, comes upon the wave of your rocking thought; her smile touches you now in age, as it never touched you in boyhood.

The image of that fair Miss Dalton, who led your fancy into such mad captivity, glides across your vision like the fragment of a crazy dream—long gone by. The country-home, where lived the grandfather of Frank, gleams kindly in the sunlight of your memory; and still,—poor, blind Fanny,—long since gathered to that rest, where her closed eyes will open upon visions of joy,—draws forth a sigh of pity.

Then, comes up that sweetest, and brightest vision of love, and the doubt and care which ran before it,—when your hope groped eagerly through your pride, and worldliness, toward the sainted purity of her, whom you knew to be—all too good; —when you trembled at the thought of your own vices, and blackness, in the presence of her, who seemed—virtue's self. And even now, your old heart bounds with joy, as you recal the first timid assurance,—that you were blessed in the possession of her love, and that you might live in her smiles.

Your thought runs like floating melody, over the calm joy that followed you through so many years—to the prattling children, who were there to bless your path. How poor, seem now your transports, as you met their childish embraces, and mingled in their childish employ;—how utterly weak, the actual, when compared with that glow of affection, which memory lends to the scene!

Yet all this is gone; and the anxieties are gone, which knit your heart so strongly to those children, and to her—the mother—anxieties which distressed you,—which you would eagerly have shunned; yet, whose memory you would not now bargain away, for a king's ransom. What were the sunlight worth, if clouds did not sometimes hide its brightness; what were the spring, or the summer if the lessons of the chilling winter did not teach us the story of their warmth?

The days are gone too, in which you may have lingered under the sweet suns of Italy,—with the cherished one beside you, and the eager children, learning new prattle, in the soft language of those Eastern lands. The evenings are gone, in which you have loitered under the trees, with those dear ones, under the light of a harvest moon, and talked of your blooming hopes, and of the stirring plans of your manhood. There are no more ambitious hopes—no more sturdy plans! Life's work has rounded into the evening that shortens labor.

And as you loiter in dreams over the wide waste of what is gone,—a mingled array of griefs and of joys—of failures, and of triumphs,—you bless God, that there has been so much of joy, belonging to your shattered life; and you pray God, with the vain fondness that belongs to a parent's heart,—that more of joy, and less of toil, may come near to the cherished ones, who bear up your hope and name.

And with your silent prayer, come back the old teachings, and vagaries of the boyish heart, in its reaches toward Heaven. You recal the old church-reckoning of your goodness: is there much more of it now, than then? Is not Heaven just as high, and the world as sadly—broad?

Alas, for the poor tale of goodness, which age brings to the memory! There may be crowning acts of benevolence, shining here and there but the margin of what has not been done, is very broad. How weak and insignificant, seems the story of life's goodness, and profit, when Death begins to slant his shadow upon our souls! How infinite, in the comparison, seems that Eternal goodness, which is crowned with mercy. How self vanishes, like a blasted thing; and only lives —if it lives at all,—in the glow of that redeeming light, which radiates from the CROSS, and the THRONE.

II.

What is Left.

BUT much as there is gone of life and of its joys,—very much remains;—very much in earnest, and very much more in hope. Still, you see visions, and you dream dreams, of the times that are to come.

Your home, and heart are left; within that home, the old Bible holds its wonted place, which was the monitor of your boyhood; and now, more than ever, it prompts those reverent reaches of the spirit, which go beyond even the track of dreams.

That cherished Madge, the partner of your life and joy, still lingers, though her step is feeble, and her eyes are dimmed;—not, as once, attracting you by any outward show of beauty; your heart glowing through the memory of a life of joy, needs no such stimulant to the affections. Your hearts are knit together by a habit of growth, and a unanimity of desire. There is less to remind of the vanities of earth, and more to quicken the hopes of a time, when body yields to spirit.

Your own poor, battered hulk wants no jaunty-trimmed craft for consort; but twin of heart, and soul, as you are twin of years, you float tranquilly toward that haven, which lies before us all.

Your children, now almost verging on maturity, bless your hearth, and home. Not one is gone. Frank indeed, that wild fellow of a youth, who has wrought your heart into perplexing anxieties again and again, as you have seen the wayward dashes of his young blood,—is often away. But his heart yet centres, where yours centres; and his absence is only a nearer, and bolder strife, with that fierce world, whose circumstances, every man of force, and energy, is born to conquer.

His return, from time to time, with that proud figure of opening manliness, and that flush of health, speaks to your affections, as you could never have believed it would. It is not for a man, who is the father of a man, to show any weakness of the heart, or any over-sensitiveness, in those ties which bind him to his kin. And yet—yet, as you sit by your fire-side with your clear, gray eye, feasting in its feebleness on that proud figure of a man,—who calls you—'father,'—and as you see his fond, and loving attentions to that one, who has been your partner in all anxieties, and joys,—there *is* a throbbing within your bosom that makes you almost wish him young again :—that you might embrace him now, as when he warbled in your rejoicing ear, those first words of love.——Ah, how little does a son know the secret and craving tenderness of a parent;—how little conception has he, of those silent bursts of fondness, and of joy, which attend his coming, and which crown his parting!

There is young Madge too,—dark-eyed, tall, with a pensive shadow resting on her face,—the very image of refinement, and of delicacy. She is thoughtful;—not breaking out, like the hoyden, flax-haired Nelly, into bursts of joy, and singing,— but stealing upon your heart, with a gentle and quiet tenderness, that diffuses itself throughout the household, like a soft zephyr of summer.

There are friends too yet left, who come in upon your evening hours; and light up the loitering time with dreamy story of the years that are gone. How eagerly you listen to some gossiping veteran friend, who with his deft words, calls up the thread of some bye-gone years of life; and with what careless, yet grateful recognition, you lapse, as it were, into the current of the past; and live over again, by your hospitable blaze, the stir, the joy, and the pride of your lost manhood.

The children of friends too, have grown upon your march; and come to welcome you with that reverent deference, which always touches the heart of age. That wild boy Will.,—the son of a dear friend—who but a little while ago, was worrying you with his boyish pranks, has now shot up into a tall, and graceful youth; and evening after evening, finds him making part of your little household group.

Does the fond old man think that *he* is all the attraction!

It may be that in your dreamy speculations, about the future of your children (for still you dream) you think that Will. may possibly become the husband of the sedate and kindly Madge. It worries you to find Nelly teasing him as she does; that mad hoyden will never be quiet; she provokes you excessively;—and yet, she is a dear creature; there is no meeting those laughing blue eyes of hers, without a smile, and an embrace.

It pleases you however to see the winning frankness, with which Madge always receives Will. And with a little of your old vanity of observation, you trace out the growth of their dawning attachment. It provokes you, to find Nelly breaking up their quiet *tête-à-têtes* with her provoking sallies; and drawing away Will. to some saunter in the garden, or to some mad gallop over the hills.

At length, upon a certain summer's day, Will. asks to see you. He approaches with a doubtful, and disturbed look; you fear that wild Nell has been teasing him with her pranks. Yet he wears, not so much an offended look, as one of fear. You wonder if it ever happened to you, to carry your hat in just that timid manner, and to wear such a shifting expression of the eye, as poor Will. wears just now? You wonder if it ever happened to you, to begin to talk with an old friend of your father's, in just that abashed way? Will. must have fallen into some sad scrape.——Well he is a good fellow, and you will help him out of it.

You look up as he goes on with his story;—you grow perplexed yourself;—you scarce believe your own ears.

——" Nelly?"—Is Will. talking of Nelly?

" Yes, sir,—Nelly."

——" What!—and you have told all this to Nelly—that you love her?"

" I have, sir."

" And she says——"

" That I must speak with you, sir."

" Bless my soul!—But she's a good girl;"—and the old man wipes his eyes.

——" Nell!—are you there?"

And she comes,—blushing, lingering, yet smiling through it all.

——" And you could deceive your old father, Nell——" (very fondly.)

Nelly only clasps your hand in both of hers.

" And so you loved Will., all the while?"

——Nelly only stoops, to drop a little kiss of pleading on your forehead.

——" Well, Nelly " (it is hard to speak roundly) " give me your hand;—here, Will.,—take it:—she's a wild girl;—be kind to her, Will.?"

" God bless you, sir!"

And Nelly throws herself, sobbing, upon your bosom.

——-" Not here,—not here, now, Nell!—Will is yonder!"

———Sobbing, sobbing still. Nelly, Nelly,—who would have thought that your merry face covered such heart of tenderness!

III.

Grief and Joy of Age.

THE winter has its piercing storms,—even as Autumn hath. Hoary age, crowned with honor, and with years, bears no immunity from suffering. It is the common heritage of us all: if it come not in the spring, or in the summer of our day, it will surely find us in the autumn, or amid the frosts of winter. It is the penalty humanity pays for pleasure; human joys will have their balance. Nature never makes false weight. The east wind is followed by a wind from the west; and every smile will have its equivalent—in a tear.

You have lived long, and joyously, with that dear one, who has made your life—a holy pilgrimage. She has seemed to lead you into ways of pleasantness, and has kindled in you—as the damps of the world came near to extinguish them,—those hopes and aspirations, which rest not in life, but soar to the realm of spirits.

You have sometimes shuddered with the thought of parting; you have trembled even at the leave-taking of a year, or—of months; and have suffered bitterly, as some danger threatened a parting—forever. That danger threatens now. Nor is it a sudden fear, to startle you into a paroxysm of dread—nothing of this. Nature is kinder,—or, she is less kind.

It is a slow, and certain approach of danger, which you read in the feeble step,—in the wan eye, lighting up from time to time, into a brightness that seems no longer of this world. You read it in the new, and ceaseless attentions of the fond child who yet blesses your home; and who conceals from you the bitterness of the coming grief.

Frank is away—over seas; and as the mother mentions that name with a tremor of love and of regret, that he is not now with you all,—you recal that other death, when you too,—were not there. Then you knew little of a parent's feeling;—now its intensity is present!

Day after day, as summer passes, she is ripening for that world where her faith, and her hope, have so long lived. Her pressure of your hand at some casual parting for a day, is full of a gentle warning —as if she said—prepare for a longer adieu!

Her language too, without direct mention, steeps your thought in the bitter certainty that she foresees her approaching doom; and that she dreads t, only so far as she dreads the grief, that will be left in her broken home. Madge—the daughter,—glides through the duties of that household, like an angel of mercy: she lingers at the sick bed—blessing, and taking blessings.

The sun shines warmly without; and through the open casement, beats warmly upon the floor within. The birds sing in the joyousness of full-robed summer; the drowsy hum of the bees, stealing sweets from the honeysuckle that bowers the window, lulls the air to a gentle quiet. Her breathing scarce breaks the summer stillness. Yet, she knows it is nearly over. Madge, too,—with features saddened, yet struggling against grief,—feels—that it is nearly over.

It is very hard to think it;—how much harder to know it! But there is no mistaking her look now—so placid, so gentle, so resigned! And her grasp of your hand—so warm—so full of meaning!

——"Madge, Madge, must it be?" And a pleasant smile lights her eye; and her grasp is warmer; and her look is—upward.

——"Must it,—must it be, dear Madge?"——A holier smile,—loftier,—lit up of angels, beams on her faded features. The hand relaxes its clasp; and you cling to it faster—harder;—joined close to the frail wreck of your love;—joined tightly—but oh, how far apart!

She is in Heaven;—and you, struggling against the grief of a lorn, old man!

But sorrow, however great it be, must be subdued in the presence of a child. Its fevered outbursts must be kept for those silent hours, when no young eyes are watching, and no young hearts will " catch the trick of grief."

When the household is quiet, and darkened;— when Madge is away from you, and your boy Frank slumbering—as youth slumbers upon sorrow;— when you are alone with God, and the night,—in that room so long hallowed by her presence, but now,—deserted—silent;—then you may yield yourself to such frenzy of tears, as your strength will let you. And in your solitary rambles through the churchyard, you can loiter of a summer's noon, over *her* fresh-made grave, and let your pent heart speak, and your spirit lean toward the Rest, where her love has led you.

Thornton—the clergyman, whose prayer over the dead, has dwelt with you, comes from time to time, to light up your solitary hearth, with his talk of the Rest—for all men. He is young, but his earnest, and gentle speech, win their way to your heart, and to your understanding. You love his counsels; you make of him a friend, whose visits are long, and often repeated.

Frank only lingers for a while; and you bid him again—adieu. It seems to you that it may well be the last; and your blessing trembles on your lip. Yet you look not with dread, but rather, with a firm trustfulness toward the day of the end. For your darling Madge, it is true, you have anx-

GRIEF AND JOY OF AGE. 267

leties; you fear to leave her lonely in the world, with no protector save the wayward Frank.

It is later August, when you call to Madge one day, to bring you the little escritoire, in which are your cherished papers;—among them is your last will and testament. Thornton has just left you; and it seems to you that his repeated kindnesses are deserving of some substantial mark of your regard.

"Maggie"—you say, "Mr. Thornton has been very kind to me."

"Very kind, father."

"I mean to leave him here, some little legacy, Maggie."

"I would not, father."

"But Madge, my daughter!"

"He is not looking for such return, father."

"But he has been very kind, Madge; I must show him some strong token of my regard. What shall it be, Maggie?"

Madge hesitates;—Madge blushes;—Madge stoops to her father's ear, as if the very walls might catch the secret of her heart;—"Would you give *me* to him, father?"

"But—my dear Madge—has he asked this?"

"Eight months ago, papa."

"And you told him——"

"That I would never leave you, so long as you lived!"

——"My own dear Madge,—come to me,—kiss me! And you love him, Maggie?"

"With all my heart, sir."

——" So like your mother,—the same figure, - the same true honest heart! It shall be as you wish, dear Madge. Only, you will not leave me in my old age ;—Eh, Maggie ? "

——" Never, father, never."

——And there she leans upon his chair ;—her arm around the old man's neck,—her other hand clasped in his; and her eyes melting with tenderness, as she gazes upon his aged face,—all radiant with joy and with hope.

IV.

The End of Dreams.

A FEEBLE old man, and a young lady, who is just now blooming into the maturity of womanhood, are toiling up a gentle slope, where the spring's sun lies warmly. The old man totters, though he leans heavily upon his cane; and he pants, as he seats himself upon a mossy rock, that crowns the summit of the slope. As he recovers breath, he draws the hand of the lady in his, and with a trembling eagerness he points out an old mansion that lies under the shadow of tall sycamores; and he says—feebly and brokenly,—— "That is it, Maggie,—the old home,—the sycamores,—the garret,—Charlie,—Nelly "——

The old man wipes his eyes. Then his hand shifts: he seems groping in darkness; but soon it rests upon a little cottage below, heavily overshadowed:—"That was it, Maggie: Madge lived there—sweet Madge,—your mother,"——

Again the old man wipes his eyes, and the lady turns away.

Presently they walk down the hill together They cross a little valley, with slow, faltering steps. The lady guides him carefully, until they reach a little graveyard.

"This must be it, Maggie, but the fence is new There it is, Maggie, under the willow,—my poor mother's grave!"

The lady weeps.

"Thank you, Madge: you did not know her, but you weep for me :—God bless you!"

The old man is in the midst of his household. It is some festive day. He holds feebly his place, at the head of the board. He utters in feeble tones —a Thanksgiving.

His married Nelly is there, with two blooming children. Frank is there with his bride. Madge— dearest of all,—is seated beside the old man, watchful of his comfort, and assisting him, as, with a shadowy dignity, he essays to do the honors of the board. The children prattle merrily : the elder ones talk of the days gone by; and the old man enters feebly—yet with floating glimpses of glee,— into the cheer, and the rejoicings.

——Poor old man, he is near his tomb! Yet his calm eye, looking upwards, seems to show no fear.

The same old man is in his chamber : he cannot

leave his chair now. Madge is beside him Nelly is there too, with her eldest-born. Madge has been reading to the old man :—it was a passage of promise—of the Bible promise.

"A glorious promise,"—says the old man feebly.

——"A promise to me,—a promise to her—poor Madge!"

"Is her picture there, Maggie?"

Madge brings it to him : he turns his head ; but the light is not strong. They wheel his chair to the window. The sun is shining brightly :—still the old man cannot see.

"It is getting dark, Maggie."

Madge looks at Nelly—wistfully—sadly.

The old man murmurs something ; and Madge stoops :——" Coming," he says,——" coming !"

Nelly brings the little child to take his hand. Perhaps it will revive him. She lifts her boy to kiss his cheek.

The old man does not stir: his eyes do not move :—they seem fixed above. The child cries as his lips touch the cold cheek:——It is a tender SPRING flower, upon the bosom of the dying WINTER!

——The old man is gone: his dream life is ended.

THE END.

www.ingramcontent.com/pod-product-compliance
Lightning Source LLC
Chambersburg PA
CBHW031943230426
43672CB00010B/2032